INSPIRE!

INSPIRE!

WHY CUSTOMERS COME BACK

JIM CHAMPY

© 2009 by James A. Champy

Pearson Education, Inc.
Publishing as FT Press
Upper Saddle River, New Jersey 07458

FT Press offers excellent discounts on this book when ordered in quantity for bulk purchases or special sales. For more information, please contact U.S. Corporate and Government Sales, 1-800-382-3419, corpsales@pearsontechgroup.com. For sales outside the U.S., please contact International Sales at international@pearson.com.

Printed in the United States of America

First Printing April 2009

ISBN-10: 0131361880
ISBN-13: 9780131361881

Pearson Education LTD.
Pearson Education Australia PTY, Limited.
Pearson Education Singapore, Pte. Ltd.
Pearson Education North Asia, Ltd.
Pearson Education Canada, Ltd.
Pearson Educación de Mexico, S.A. de C.V.
Pearson Education—Japan
Pearson Education Malaysia, Pte. Ltd.

Vice President, Publisher
Tim Moore

Associate Publisher and Director of Marketing
Amy Neidlinger

Editorial Assistant
Pamela Boland

Operations Manager
Gina Kanouse

Digital Marketing Manager
Julie Phifer

Publicity Manager
Laura Czaja

Assistant Marketing Manager
Megan Colvin

Cover Designer
the Ingredient

Design Manager
Sandra Schroeder

Managing Editor
Kristy Hart

Senior Project Editor
Lori Lyons

Copy Editor
Krista Hansing Editorial Services

Proofreader
San Dee Phillips

Indexer
Erika Millen

Senior Compositor
Jake McFarland

Manufacturing Buyer
Dan Uhrig

Library of Congress Cataloging-in-Publication Data

Champy, James, 1942-
  Inspire! : why customers come back / Jim Champy.
      p. cm.
   ISBN-10: 0-13-136188-0 (hardback : alk. paper)
   ISBN-13: 978-0-13-136188-1 (hardback : alk. paper) 1. Marketing. 2.
Consumer education. 3. Customer relations--Management. 4. Authenticity
(Philosophy) I. Title.
  HF5415.C48244 2009
  658.8--dc22
                          2008043337

This book is dedicated to Ron Christman, Tom Waite, and John Thompson—three of my business associates from whom I learned so much about inspiring customers with ideas.

CONTENTS

Introduction 2

Chapter 1   From Tired to Inspired 6

Chapter 2   What Could Be More Inspiring Than a Crusade? . . 22

Chapter 3   What Could Be More Inspiring Than
Convenience with Economy? 38

Chapter 4   What Could Be More Inspiring Than a
Trusted Channel? 56

Chapter 5   What Could Be More Inspiring Than
Simplifying Complexity? 74

Chapter 6   What Could Be More Inspiring Than Honesty? 90

Chapter 7   What Could Be More Inspiring Than Being
Your Own Customer? 108

Chapter 8   What Could Be More Inspiring Than
Enthusiastic Customers? 122

Chapter 9   What Could Be More Inspiring Than the
Melding of Cool and Sport? 138

Epilogue 152

Index 156

ACKNOWLEDGMENTS

As always, my best work is done in association with others. For this book and the others in this series, my thanks go to the talented editors and researchers at Wordworks, Inc.: Donna Sammons Carpenter, Maurice Coyle, Ruth Hlavacek, Larry Martz, Molly Sammons Morris, Cindy Sammons, Robert Shnayerson, and Robert W. Stock—and Helen Rees and Joan Mazmanian of the Helen Rees Literary Agency. I am also deeply appreciative of the efforts of my publisher, Tim Moore, and all his colleagues at Pearson: Amy Neidlinger, Megan Colvin, Julie Phifer, Sandra Schroeder, Lori Lyons, Jake McFarland, Erika Millen, Krista Hansing, and San Dee Phillips. I would also like to thank my very capable assistant Dee Dee Haggerty.

Finally, as always, I am grateful to my wife, Lois, and my son, Adam, for their support, advice, and tolerance when I write. They keep me focused on what truly matters in life.

ABOUT THE AUTHOR

Jim Champy is one of the leading management and business thinkers of our time. His first best seller, *Reengineering the Corporation*, remains the bible for executing process change. His second book, *Reengineering Management*, another best seller, was recognized by *Business Week* as one of the most important books of its time. Champy's latest book, *OUTSMART!*, shows how to achieve breakthrough growth by consistently outsmarting your competition by identifying six powerful new ways to compete in even the toughest marketplace.

Champy is also an experienced manager and advisor. He is currently the Chairman of Consulting for Perot Systems. He speaks and writes with the authority of real business experience and brings pragmatism to the world of business. In this new series of books, Champy looks at what's working today for high-growth businesses. Champy observes that there is not much new in management, but there is a lot new in business—and a lot to learn from what's new.

THIS IS THE SECOND BOOK IN A SERIES
OF COMPACT VOLUMES ON THE KEY
TOPICS OF STRATEGY, MARKETING,
MANAGING PEOPLE, AND OPERATIONS.
TAKEN TOGETHER, THESE VOLUMES
DELIVER PRACTICAL ADVICE ON
HOW TO SUCCEED IN TODAY'S BRAVE
NEW WORLD OF BUSINESS. THAT'S
BECAUSE THEY ARE ROOTED IN
THE ACTUAL EXPERIENCES AND
INSIGHTS OF A SELECT GROUP OF
COMPANIES THAT HAVE FOUND NEW
AND BETTER WAYS TO INNOVATE AND
GROW IN SPITE OF OUR CHALLENGING
ECONOMIC ENVIRONMENT.

INTRODUCTION

In *Outsmart!*, the first book of the series, I drew metaphorically from Charles Darwin's theories of survival:

- ▶ Species always breed beyond available resources.

- ▶ Those species with favorable variations have a greater chance of survival and pass on their variations to their offspring.

- ▶ Adapted species force out weaker ones, producing whole new species.

Applying these theories to business, Darwin might say that companies tend to breed beyond their available pool of customers; that companies with innovative strategies have a better chance of survival; and that such companies force out weaker rivals, creating whole new business models.

Outsmart! describes and analyzes the strategies of successful, fast-growing organizations. *Inspire!* picks up where *Outsmart!* leaves off, showing how these kinds of organizations have been able to increase their market share.

All of the companies described in this series have passed through a rigorous filter: They've grown more than 15 percent a year for the past three or more years. My initial assumption was that businesses expanding at these rates must be doing something right—and worth knowing about. My research has confirmed that assumption, as the examples in this book will illustrate.

I did not begin this project expecting to find a single driver of extraordinary growth, a single source for great strategies, or a single formula for retaining customers—nor did I find such. But all the companies in *Outsmart!* and *Inspire!* do share a set of special traits. I consistently found these similarities:

▶ Company-wide ambition for steady growth and stellar performance.

▶ Intuition valued above tradition.

▶ Focus on markets the company can serve best.

▶ Decisions driven by customer needs.

▶ Risk calmly accepted as necessity.

▶ Innovation viewed as everyone's business.

▶ Behavior governed by culture, not imposed by rigid rules.

▶ Work is taken seriously but is nearly always fun.

The companies in *Inspire!* share one additional trait: a fidelity to long expressed beliefs. These companies remain true to themselves. They consistently uphold their own values in their products, services, and actions. They are what they say they are—that is, they are authentic. You will find more about authenticity and its particular importance today in Chapter 1.

You will also experience the quality of authenticity in each company described in this book. And you will see that these companies have a purpose that goes beyond merely selling their product or service. Simply put, they have a higher calling. I hope they will inspire you, just as they have inspired their customers.

LIKE A MILLION OTHER HOPEFULS, BEN POPKEN ARRIVED IN NEW YORK ON A GREYHOUND BUS FROM HIS NATIVE DENVER AND GRABBED THE FIRST AVAILABLE JOB—BICYCLE MESSENGER. SURVIVING MANHATTAN'S BRUTAL TRAFFIC, HE EARNED ENOUGH TO BUY A DECENT SUIT AND SNAG A SAFER JOB—GOFER AT AN ONLINE MARKETING FIRM. IN HIS SPARE TIME, HE WROTE ONLINE SATIRES OF FOOLISH ADVERTISING CAMPAIGNS.

CHAPTER 1
FROM TIRED TO INSPIRED

In 2006, Popken posted his barbs at Consumerist.com, which
carries the tagline "Shoppers Bite Back." He impressed Nick
Denton, the blog tycoon who runs Gawker Media, and owner
of Consumerist. Denton quickly hired Popken as Consumerist's
editor.

Under Popken's direction, Consumerist has become a
powerhouse. Each day, it showcases approximately 30 new
complaints sent in by readers: This company refuses to cover a
repair to my laptop, which is still under warranty; that business
won't let me cancel my deceased brother's phone contract;
these manufacturers have reduced the size of their products but
not their price. (Popken calls this widespread phenomenon the
Grocery Shrink Ray.)

Such entries, along with advice for coping with laggard call
centers and other corporate failings, attract more than 15
million visitors a month. Consumerist is frequently cited by
mainstream media, including *The New York Times*, *The Wall
Street Journal*, and *BusinessWeek*. It's also high on the list of
major bookmarking sites such as Digg.com, and its multiple
links with other blogs spread its contents across the Internet.
Many companies, including Dell and Sprint, regularly monitor
Consumerist and quickly respond to comments about their
products and operations.

In his person—and in the nature of his Web site—Ben Popken is
a poster child for the genesis of this book. He and Consumerist
are emblematic of a seismic shift in the marketplace—a basic
revision, even reversal, of the buyer-seller relationship.

Customers of every age and income watch business with doubting eyes. The bigger and costlier a full-page advertisement, the less seriously people take it. Many routinely mute television commercials or, thanks to digital video recorders, simply fast-forward through them. Millions sit in constant judgment of sloppy companies, as if they were jurors wearing signs emblazoned "We Will Not Be Fooled."

Accessible information abounds. The Internet is a cornucopia of consumer intelligence, enabling anyone to learn far more about companies and their products than the businesses ever imagined or intended. Customers can easily research any company's labor practices, carbon footprint, fair trade policies, and charitable contributions. They can get the latest details about products by checking out blogs such as Consumerist or comparing notes with other shoppers on social networking sites.

If you have any doubts about the changes transforming the marketplace, hear this: A recent study by market research firm Yankelovich found that more than half of adult Americans believe they know more about the products and services they shop for than the salespeople in stores. In another study, 51 percent of respondents said that the most trusted source of product information was "a person like themselves."

A RECENT STUDY BY MARKET RESEARCH FIRM YANKELOVICH FOUND THAT MORE THAN HALF OF ADULT AMERICANS BELIEVE THEY KNOW MORE ABOUT THE PRODUCTS AND SERVICES THEY SHOP FOR THAN THE SALESPEOPLE IN STORES.

How does all this affect your business? In one sense, it means that you no longer fully control your company's image and message—your customers do. But in another sense, it means that you can vastly improve your image by changing your behavior in ways that will be noticed and appreciated faster than ever. The Web empowers customers, but it also empowers companies.

Where did today's knowledgeable, independent consumer come from? Constant social interaction via cellphone and computer has led people to search out consensus. They're team players, forever seeking advice from and offering advice to a long list of correspondents, and sharing their life experiences in blogs and instant messages. They're distrustful of information from outside their circle and will go to great lengths to avoid traditional advertising messages.

The new skeptics have their own ways of finding out what to buy and their own expectations of how companies should behave. For businesses to scoff at such views is counterproductive. If you suspect it's time to resurrect that old cliché "The customer is always right," you're on the right track.

To compete in today's environment (is there really any choice?), businesses need a radically different strategy. You won't find it in those business schools that are mired in orthodoxy, and management theory has little to offer. Yet the needed approach already exists and is being field-tested in the real world—out in the marketplace where smart, imaginative people are learning to cope with the new reality. And thrive in it.

I have been working to identify these people and their companies. You'll find many of them in this book, along with concrete, practical advice on how to apply their discoveries. You'll also find new vocabulary. Most of the words marketers use to describe their connection to customers are now lifeless or irrelevant. We need an active verb to capture the spirit and substance of whatever must be done to regain customer loyalty. The verb I've chosen—*inspire*—conveys the act of breathing life into something moribund and igniting latent energy to help it soar. With this meaning, I expect businesses to inspire people by offering products and services so authentic and transparent—and so in tune with today's customers' best instincts—that loyalty follows, not just once, but for lifetimes.

IT'S NOT JUST A CAMPAIGN

Companies have traditionally thought of marketing in terms of a campaign: Get your product defined, segment your audience, appeal to each segment, craft the messages, select the advertising medium, and go for the customer.

That approach is insufficient to inspire today's customer. You must start thinking in terms of mutual interest and a common cause, not the hype and spin of a conventional campaign. You must be seen as an advocate for goods and services truly worth buying and using. You must promise value and excellence. And if you don't deliver, your business might not last long.

As you will soon learn, all of this book's new strategies for attracting customers have the aura of a reform movement.

They don't just sell; they inspire. You will read about companies breaking into new territory, energized by leaders who fervently believe in the worth of their work. Some of their products and services are radically new, not just incremental improvements to what customers can already find. These companies challenge the cold calculations of their industries and plow new ground.

Such efforts don't take shape overnight. It takes clear analysis and solid preparation, plus drive and spirit. So as you begin this book, you might want to consider the following four questions:

- *Is your product or service really new, and does it go beyond making what already exists in your markets only slightly better?* A "me, too" product that's a little less expensive won't cut it in the market for very long. You must deliver something really new or substantially improved.

- *Does your approach appeal to your customers' values?* It's one thing to deliver a tangible good. But turning it into something that inspires customers requires broad support to build a business of any scale. A truly inspiring strategy is based on beliefs that engage sufficient customers only if those beliefs are widely shared.

- *Are you prepared to challenge accepted industry assumptions?* All the companies in this book broke the rules of their industry in some way. Their courage paid off, but risk was implicit in what they did.

- *Do you have the persistence to stay in the game?* You can't build a business that inspires customers in weeks or months—it takes years. Some of the companies in this book achieved early success, but it took years for them to hone their business models so that they could be assured of the continued customer loyalty.

If the answer to all these questions is "yes," this book is for you. In the chapters ahead, I describe companies that have seized the opportunity to inspire their customers. From these examples, I draw lessons that are applicable to organizations of every kind and size. Those lessons include

▸ *You can inspire by presenting your company or your products as allied to a compelling cause.* The opportunities are substantial, although you must proceed with care. Never risk any hint that you're not acting in good faith. The slightest appearance of hypocrisy on your part is likely to unite both sides of the cause—believers and detractors—in trying to sneer you out of business. Chapter 2, "What Could Be More Inspiring Than a Crusade?" describes how Gary Hirshberg, founder and CE-Yo of Stonyfield Farm, the world's largest producer of organic yogurt, avoided those pitfalls by using his product as a forthright messenger for environmental causes.

▸ *People everywhere feel more stressed by running short of time.* Combine convenience with low price, and you inspire customers with a winning sales formula. Chapter 3, "What Could Be More Inspiring Than Convenience with Economy?" is about an authentic crusader for convenience—Zipcar, the Boston-based car-sharing company that now serves carless city dwellers from San Francisco to Toronto. Zipcar targets a specific neighborhood, parks cars within a seven-minute walk, and makes sure that local member-customers never lack wheels. Its convenience includes free insurance, maintenance, and gasoline. You can also choose among diverse models, from a VW to a BMW, all equipped with GPS and XM Satellite radios. The company never stops elaborating on its convenience pitch, constantly surprising, delighting, and, yes, inspiring its customers.

▶ *Even the most customer-focused companies often overlook the bad habits of their distribution partners.* An example is when the Big Three automakers allowed slick dealers to alienate would-be customers. Chapter 4, "What Could Be More Inspiring Than a Trusted Channel?" explains how companies and their partners can forge creative relationships that captivate customers and boost profits for all concerned.

Success depends on whether you and your partners are willing to understand and share your business models for everyone's benefit. By following that inspired and inspiring formula, MemberHealth, an Ohio company helping the elderly with drug discounts, transformed itself into the fastest-growing company in the United States. In just three years, it became a Medicare Part D prescription drug insurer, with revenues that soared 20,000-fold to $1.24 billion. Founder Chuck Hallberg did it by finding and partnering with organizations that his competitors largely ignored—the 63,000 mom-and-pop pharmacies that serve smaller communities.

▶ *For all its contributions to our pleasure and well-being, technology has its discontents.* Many people have trouble learning to use new gadgets, and everyone encounters technical problems from time to time. Trying to get help can be trying in the extreme—wasted hours struggling to use self-help directions, and more wasted hours waiting for a customer service representative to pick up. Companies that engage with these customers in the most simple and direct manner have a major advantage over their competitors.

In the online world, Go Daddy, the inspiring company highlighted in Chapter 5, "What Could Be More Inspiring Than Simplifying Complexity?" specializes in making the complex simple. It sells low-price domain names and software to make it easy to set up Web sites. Customers contacting its call center can dial one number, receive immediate help, and pay nothing for the extra service. If the first respondent can't handle the customer's problem—an unusual occurrence—higher-level technical people stand ready to solve it. The company is so dedicated to simplifying operations that it assigns a team of experts to take permanent custody of every major new product. Everyone knows who specializes in what, thereby eliminating the long delays in other companies when people flit from one product to another while customers fret, fume, and age.

▶ *Not a day goes by without bleak news of yet another company collapse or scandal.* Public confidence in business is at a historic low. But that very fact presents a little-recognized business opportunity. Consumers are looking for companies whose products and behavior they can trust. To inspire them, your company has to be seen as—and be—a paragon of honest products and transparent dealing. Everything is open to customer scrutiny, from your charitable contributions to your personnel policies. The customers you attract with honesty tend to be particularly picky. It's essential to follow any changes in their desires and tastes—take your cue from them.

You might also take your cue from Honest Tea, an uncommon enterprise based in Bethesda, Maryland, that is now America's biggest purveyor of organic bottled tea. As Chapter 6, "What Could Be More Inspiring Than Honesty?" reports, Honest Tea started out as a glint in the eyes of a Yale University business school professor and one of his students. They discovered that, except for water, every naturally sweetened drink on the market at the time was loaded with the equivalent of 10 or more teaspoons of sugar—an invitation to diabetes, obesity, and problem teeth.

The two founders created a drink that used a higher grade of tea and far less sugar. They put their signatures on the bottle, vouching their honesty in all things—a promise they have kept, however much it hurt. For example, the labels were at the printer when they found that the sweetener in a brand new drink they'd called Zero actually added 3.5 calories to each bottle. Government regulations allowed rounding labels and ads for anything less than 5 calories to 0, but the founders changed the name. And in the long run, they found that honesty has been the most rewarding policy—financially and emotionally.

▶ *We often hear about a promising new product that never takes off because it doesn't really match the needs of the target customers.* One way around that potential disaster is to design a product or service that precisely fits one or more of your own needs—start out by targeting yourself as your own customer.

It would be hard to find a more inspiring example of this approach than the moving story of Two Little Hands Productions, a mixed-media company based in Midvale, Utah, that is the subject of Chapter 7, "What Could Be More Inspiring Than Being Your Own Customer?"

When Rachel and Aaron Coleman discovered that their one-year-old daughter, Leah, was deaf, they taught her American Sign Language. Leah's vocabulary and reading skills soon far exceeded those of children her age with normal hearing. Rachel's sister, Emilie Brown, and her husband, Derek, decided to teach their son, Alex, to sign so that he could converse with his cousin. When Alex was just nine months old, he began signing back, more than a year before Brown expected to be able to communicate with her baby. As you'll see, greater personal challenges awaited the Colemans. But out of the sisters' hardships came the realization that they had an insight they could share with others, and make a profit along the way: Parents and children can use sign language to communicate at a much earlier age than children can talk. The sisters made a video showing parents how to go about it, and then more videos. Within a few years, Two Little

Hands had revenues of more than $3 million, all because the sisters were able to use their own experience to inspire their customers.

▶ *Your best salesperson is a customer who is so pleased with your product or service that he or she can't stop praising it to the world at large.* But getting such volunteer marketers to pitch for your product or service is no small feat.

It takes great patience and perseverance to inspire a corps of selling customers. Those are qualities that Ed Fisher has in abundance, as Chapter 8, "What Could Be More Inspiring Than Enthusiastic Customers?" shows. It took him years to develop his Big Green Egg ceramic barbecue grill, based on an ancient Japanese utensil, to the point that it met his own quality standards. It took more years for him to connect with and gather the many thousands of loyal, talkative customers who have spread the word about the Egg far and wide. In addition to the loving care customers receive at the call center and in responses to their mail, biggreenegg.com features a forum where hundreds of Eggheads, as they call themselves, share cooking tips and recipes every day.

▶ *Knowing which parts of your legacy to keep and which to jettison is crucial to reviving a former highflier that has fallen back to earth.* You'll bore your customers, not inspire them, if you can't figure out how to change while staying the same—and that's doubly true for a company with one foot in sport and one in fashion.

Jochen Zeitz, the man who has brought German sports-shoemaker Puma back to life, first performed old-fashioned triage on his loss-ridden, debt-burdened patient, cutting employees and manufacturing costs by moving production to Asia. Then, with the company back on sound footing, he set about designing a strategy that would inspire customers to form long-lasting bonds with Puma. Chapter 9, "What Could Be More Inspiring Than the Melding of Cool and Sport?" traces the path of a makeover that has allowed the company to hold onto and even embellish its reputation as a producer of shoes for serious sport—Olympic sprinting sensation Usain Bolt broke records wearing golden Pumas—while also attracting a new following among fashionistas taken with the edgy styles conceived by a stable of trendy young designers.

By focusing on "sports lifestyle," a new term coined by Zeitz, Puma has moved into contention for third place behind market leaders Nike and Adidas without ever bloodying itself in the sneaker war. It performed this feat by expanding the playing field beyond athletic shoes to include auto-racing suits, driving shoes, sailing clothes, and other sports apparel that appeals to upscale customers. Zeitz says his strategy is to lead, not follow. And by fusing fashion and performance, Puma has lifted its gross profit margin above 52 percent. How's that for inspiration?

AUTHENTICITY IS THE MOTHER OF INSPIRATION

Many companies profess appealing values, typically in the form of catchy slogans. But the slogans are often superficial and keep changing, negating any aura of inspiration, much less sincerity. Inspirational companies are quite different. What makes them special is their fidelity to long-expressed beliefs. These companies remain true to themselves. They consistently uphold their own values in their products, services, and actions. They are what they say they are, at all times—they are authentic.

Authenticity is the key to nurturing a solid customer base. You might get the first order by fooling a customer once, but forget any further business unless you strive to deliver the quality you profess to offer. Authenticity pays.

AUTHENTICITY IS THE KEY TO NURTURING A SOLID CUSTOMER BASE. YOU MIGHT GET THE FIRST ORDER BY FOOLING A CUSTOMER ONCE, BUT FORGET ANY FURTHER BUSINESS UNLESS YOU STRIVE TO DELIVER THE QUALITY YOU PROFESS TO OFFER. AUTHENTICITY PAYS.

Unfortunately, the word *authenticity* means little to many contemporary managers, who might use the word but don't grasp what it takes for a company to behave authentically.

The issue of authenticity goes well beyond a product or service. It also applies to how a company acts in all ways and in all relationships. In business, authenticity is the highest form of integrity, and those who lack it had best choose either a character transplant or a career change.

A company is always tested when confronted by a decision that pits sticking to its values against maximizing its profits—that's the moment of truth.

Business history provides ample examples of authentic behavior. They include Johnson & Johnson's 1982 decision to remove potentially contaminated Tylenol from shelves at a huge financial loss (but high moral gain) to protect the public and uphold its own values. More recently, the S. C. Johnson Company has demonstrated unusual commitment to environment-friendly products and manufacturing.

A company that emphasizes authenticity challenges itself to behave accordingly. If you drift from your expressed values today, the Internet's morality police are very likely to nab your reputation.

The other challenge that an authentic company faces is keeping true in all its actions as it grows. This challenge is more relevant today as companies become global, with dispersed operations involving hundreds of people making thousands of decisions that present moments of truth or untruth. The only prescription I have for dealing with this phenomenon is to be very explicit about your company's beliefs, values, and practices—and not tolerate any variances. I have often heard the argument that a country's culture should allow for different corporate behaviors, but that argument cannot be sustained if you want to be true to one set of corporate values. Local cultures can help you determine local differences for products and how you go to market in different regions, but local cultures should not be an excuse for allowing deviant behavior to undercut your authenticity.

I HAVE OFTEN HEARD THE ARGUMENT THAT A COUNTRY'S CULTURE SHOULD ALLOW FOR DIFFERENT CORPORATE BEHAVIORS, BUT THAT ARGUMENT CANNOT BE SUSTAINED IF YOU WANT TO BE TRUE TO ONE SET OF CORPORATE VALUES.

Of all the qualities and characteristics that I have described both in my previous book, *Outsmart!*, and in this book, authenticity might be the easiest quality to adopt—if you have the courage to be honest about your business. It starts with being clear about what your company stands for and then aligning behavior with your beliefs. And being authentic can actually make business life easier. When you're clear on what you value, the answers to tough questions become clearer. And you will keep your customers because they trust you.

Authenticity also illuminates a company's sense of purpose. It literally shines a light on what a company aspires to do. And authenticity underlies much of what the inspiring companies in this book have accomplished. You can do the same. It begins with your willingness to seize today's huge opportunities and to inspire those millions who yearn to be inspired themselves.

GARY HIRSHBERG WAS A GRASS-GREEN ECOLOGIST AND UNABASHED IDEALIST, SINGLE-MINDEDLY DEDICATED TO SAVING THE PLANET, WHEN HE HAD AN EPIPHANY. IT WOULD CHANGE HIS CAREER AND LAND HIM ON THE LEADING EDGE OF A NEW WAVE OF EARTH-FRIENDLY ENTERPRISES. AND WHEN HE LEARNED TO ENGAGE HIS CUSTOMERS BY ENLISTING THEM IN HIS CRUSADE, HE HAD AN UNBEATABLE FORMULA FOR SUCCESS.

CHAPTER 2
WHAT COULD BE MORE INSPIRING THAN A CRUSADE?

Hirshberg found his calling long before his moment of illumination. As a boy in New Hampshire, he was entranced by the Technicolor wastewater that flashed from green to yellow to red as it gushed into the Suncook River from his family's shoe factory. But then he learned that the mesmerizing hues were the product of pollution, and that pollution in all its forms was endangering the planet. Before long, Hirshberg was a fervent environmentalist who earned a degree in environmental science and began traveling the world to build windmills and teach others how to build them, too.

By the late 1970s, he was executive director of the proudly named New Alchemy Institute, an ecological research center in Woods Hole, Massachusetts. Its solar-heated, wind-powered greenhouse produced enough food to feed ten people three meals a day, year-round, showing that food production could be sustainable without using fossil fuels, pesticides, herbicides, or chemical fertilizer. Huge fish tanks soaked up sunlight during the day, and the water produced enough heat to warm the place at night. Each tank supported about 100 pounds of fish per year, and the fish waste fertilized the plants that were then turned into fish food. Even in midwinter, the greenhouse was warm enough to grow bananas, figs, papayas, and other fruits. The New Alchemy Institute was earnest, ingenious, and successful. Nearly 25,000 admiring visitors trooped through it every year.

In 1982, Hirshberg's cozy world was shattered when he visited the Land Pavilion at Disney's EPCOT Center in Orlando, Florida, and encountered Kraft Foods' vision of the farm of the future. Kraft's dream display was an ecologist's nightmare: Plants were grown hydroponically, suspended in plastic tubes, while streams of petrochemical fertilizer, herbicides, and pesticides washed their naked roots. Not a grain of actual soil was to be found. Anything but sustainable, this kind of farming relied on plundering the Earth for carbon-based chemicals stored as fossil fuels eons ago, and then spewing carbon back into the air. And for Hirshberg, fossil-fueled insult was added to chemical-injected injury by the center's conventional lighting and air conditioning. He was doubly appalled when he realized that Kraft foisted this unsustainable fantasy on more people every day than heard New Alchemy's message in a full year.

Hirshberg felt powerless and outgunned. Faced with Kraft's smooth marketing and publicity machine, well oiled by its huge stash of corporate dollars, he and his green colleagues seemed little more than puny innocents preaching to the already converted and making little headway in an uncaring world. Against such odds, how could they possibly save the planet?

That's when inspiration struck, and he blurted it out loud: "I have to become Kraft."

As Hirshberg explained years later, he was still convinced that "Kraft was crazy and only sustainable practices could save the planet." But now he knew that for him and his like-minded brethren to be heard outside their own, already-committed congregation of true believers, they needed the clout of profitable and powerful businesses behind them. What Hirshberg didn't know, though, was how his work to save the environment would evolve into an effective way to engage customers.

About Organic

What is Organic?

Organic refers to the way agricultural products- food and fiber- are grown and processed. It is an ecological system that at its core relies on a healthy rich soil to produce strong plants that resist pests and diseases. Organic farming prohibits the use of toxic and persistent chemicals in favor of more "earth-friendly" practices that work in harmony with nature. In the case of livestock, antibiotics are prohibited, opting instead for preventative measures for keeping animals healthy and productive. Organic production also prohibits the use of genetically modified organisms (GMO's).

Organic farmers work in harmony with nature.

Organic practices include:

- Crop rotation- alternating the types of crops grown in each field, which in turn prevents the depletion of the soil. Pests are also managed through crop rotation by eliminating breeding grounds built year after year with a continuous crop.
- Planting cover crops, such as clover adds nutrients to the soil, prevents weeds, and increases organic matter in the soil. Soil with high organic matter resists erosion and holds water better, requiring less irrigation. Studies have shown that organic crops fare better than non-organic crops in times of drought and stress.
- Releasing beneficial insects to prey on pests helps to eliminate the need for chemical insecticides that can remain in the soil for years or leach into our water supply.
- Adding composted manure and plant wastes helps the soil retain moisture and nutrients. Just as falling leaves return nutrients to forest soil, composting replenishes the soil.
- Preventing illness and maintaining strong animals through good nutrition and minimal stress are key to successful organic livestock farming.

Organic Practices mean:

- No pesticides to contaminate our soil and water or injure farm workers!
- No chemical fertilizers to runoff and contaminate our rivers, lakes, oceans and drinking water!
- A healthier and more sustainable environment for us all!

Stonyfield takes organic seriously—from the soil to the customer, organic is much more than a label on its products. Organic is a belief that the company practices and teaches, as evidenced by how the requirements for being organic are described on its website: **www.stonyfield.com**.

Hirshberg left New Alchemy, went home to New Hampshire, took some business classes, and became a partner in a quixotic yogurt-making start-up that, in time, enabled him to prove the correctness of his epiphany. Today Stonyfield Farm is the world's largest maker of organic yogurt—a company that has grown by more than 27 percent a year for 18 straight years and regularly turns a handsome profit. Hirshberg, who calls himself the CE-Yo, still runs the business.

Like any small company, Stonyfield lurched from crisis to crisis in its first years, repeatedly facing make-or-break decisions. Perhaps the most pivotal decision was how to engage customers.

Hirshberg and his partner, Samuel Kaymen, were convinced from the outset that their yogurt was its own best marketer: One taste would tell any yogurt lover that this was a truly exceptional product. The problem was determining how to get people to taste it. The pair had no money for advertising or conventional marketing. Organic food stores might be persuaded to carry Stonyfield yogurt, but they were few in number back then and their reach ended with the minuscule market of health fanatics. Luckily, a friend of Hirshberg's was an executive at the Stop & Shop supermarket chain, and he wrangled a test promotion that gave Stonyfield dairy case space in five stores and permission to hand out samples to customers for 12 weeks.

Even that tiny inroad wasn't easily navigable for Hirshberg and Kaymen: They and their families were the entire crew at Stonyfield in those days—milking 19 cows twice a day, making yogurt, sweet-talking nervous bankers, and handling all the paperwork. Unless they could persuade a neighbor or Kaymen's wife, Louise, to do the milking, they had to take turns passing out the samples and pitching their amateur sales spiel to customers at one of the five stores. Plain yogurt was their only product at first, so they flavored each sample spoonful with a drizzle of locally produced maple syrup. Their total sales kit was made up of a folding table, a homemade sign, the yogurt, the maple syrup, a stash of paper napkins and plastic spoons, and an apron.

The yogurt makers pressed their samples on every passerby—shoppers, store operators, dairy managers, even brand representatives checking their shelf stock. Hirshberg later quipped that he and Kaymen had "all the innocence of Cub Scouts selling chances for a free car wash." But somehow it worked: Their missionary zeal about planet-saving, sustainable business practices combined with the yogurt's extraordinary quality attracted enough buyers to persuade Stop & Shop to carry the yogurt in every one of the chain's several hundred stores throughout New England.

Best of all, the partners had made what Hirshberg came to call Stonyfield Farm's "handshake with the customer." The handshake wasn't physical contact; it was instead an implied contract—a guarantee that the yogurt was both delicious and made in a way that furthered the cause of saving the planet. It was pure and organic or all natural; the milk used was free of preservatives, and most of it came from cows that hadn't been exposed to chemicals, pesticides, and drugs. Happy shoppers soon passed the word about Stonyfield to their friends, and the brand began to take off.

Chicago was the scene of one of Stonyfield's biggest successes.
A major supermarket chain offered to give Hirshberg space
in its dairy cases if he could quadruple Stonyfield's market
share to 3 percent within three months. But he was told that
achieving that kind of growth required a $10 million advertising
campaign. Stonyfield didn't have the money; instead, it
passed out 85,000 free cups of yogurt to the city's public
transit riders, along with coupons that read: "We salute your
commute! Thanks for doing your part to help save the planet."
Accompanying brochures informed riders that every person
who commutes by train instead of car prevents 44 pounds
of particulates from flooding into the atmosphere annually.
Only three days into the campaign, a freshet of newspaper and
television coverage bubbled up, lifting Stonyfield's market share
to 2.5 percent and assuring that the goal would be reached. The
whole effort cost under $100,000.

Hirshberg used a variant of the same technique to invade the
Houston market—but in a city with hardly any public transit,
Hirshberg had to reach—and engage—drivers. He theorized
that many people feel at least a little bit guilty about their
impact on the planet, and they would be glad to know they
could do something to lessen the blow. So Stonyfield enlisted
Houston's drivers in its crusade by reminding them to keep their
tires properly inflated to save gasoline. Brandishing a Texas-size
sign proclaiming, "We Support Inflation," the Stonyfield crew
waved in curious drivers at a busy intersection, pumped up
their tires, and explained that if every car's tires were properly
inflated, our national fuel efficiency would increase by 2 miles
per gallon of gasoline. They said the savings would equal the
potential oil production from the Alaska National Wildlife

Refuge. Drivers also got a free cup of yogurt and a tire gauge with the Stonyfield logo. Again, Stonyfield's clever promotion won it news media attention and a healthy rise in market share.

Sampling is a powerful way to turn a contact into a customer, Hirshberg points out, because it opens a path to the figurative handshake—the emotional connection—that creates true customer engagement. In Stonyfield's case, he says, customers pay a few extra pennies for a cup of yogurt to know that the producer is doing "what's right for the health and well-being of themselves and their families, our farmer suppliers, and the planet." And with that knowledge, they can feel that they, too, are doing the right thing in buying the yogurt.

Stonyfield's method of educating its customers about its planet-friendly initiatives is both ingenious and self-evident. It puts environmental and other messages on its yogurt container lids—more than 100 million of them every year. The messages vary monthly, sometimes quizzing customers or inviting them to join environmental initiatives—and sometimes directly exhorting them to measure up: "Your car choice makes a difference. Live larger, drive smaller," urged one lid.

From the beginning, Hirshberg and Kaymen used their cartons to send messages to customers. One quart container promoted Kaymen's Rural Education Center, which predated the yogurt operation and aimed to teach sustainable farming methods and recruit new organic farmers. The back of the carton proclaimed the company's "reverence for life" and said its cows received "lots of tender loving care" and were fed a wholesome diet free of chemicals and pesticides.

Stonyfield has also used the lids to mobilize political pressure for the cause. A few years ago, it printed a lid for customers to sign and send to their representatives in Congress: "I believe in efficient government, but not at the expense of my children's future. If you vote against the planet, I won't vote for you." According to Richard "Dick" Gephardt, the House Democratic leader at the time, 15,000 of those lids found their way to Capitol Hill.

Stonyfield.com also reinforces customer engagement by posting environmental news and messages, and updates on the company's donations to the cause. Its "Have a Cow" feature lets kids become make-believe co-owners of cows on farms that supply Stonyfield (after the company outgrew its own herd, it began contracting for milk from organic farmers). A new "owner" downloads a photo and history of a real cow and gets quarterly updates on its health and activities, along with news of happenings on the farm where the cow lives.

Stonyfield's marketing is about "making our customers feel good about us and our product," Hirshberg says. The company supports causes that consumers care about and invests in educational initiatives that will help improve and sustain the planet. "And even if they don't think that Stonyfield is making their lives better," he explains, "we believe they will have a sense of well-being that, at some innate level, will connect them to us and our yogurt."

Clearly, the marketing works and Stonyfield's other counterintuitive tactics further engage customers. For example, by sharing the company's wide-ranging activities on

Stonyfield.com, customers learned that when the company's wastewater overburdened the local municipal facilities, Hirshberg pitched in to build the company's own pretreatment plant. Typically, he opted for a less conventional but more efficient anaerobic system. It cost 15 percent more than a conventional plant to build, but it produces 90 percent less solid sludge, uses 40 percent less energy, and generates methane as a by-product that fuels the process. The plant will save $3.6 million during the system's first 10 years. Similarly, by improving efficiency in the plant, including updating lighting, installing good insulation systems, and updating heating systems with natural gas-burning boilers with sophisticated controls, Stonyfield saved 46 million kilowatt hours during a 10-year span—enough to power 4,500 homes for a year. The savings to Stonyfield was a cool $1.7 million.

Even when environmentally friendly investment sounds financially foolish, it can turn out to be profitable. In 2004, for example, Hirshberg spent a few hundred thousand dollars to put a rooftop solar array on his New Hampshire factory. Oil was much cheaper then, and the payback time was more than 20 years. He forged ahead anyway, because he wanted to underscore the company's environmental mission. In today's environment with high oil prices, it's not a stretch to see that the payback time will be faster. Hirshberg's single-minded emphasis on reducing waste has paid off handsomely as well. Ditching plastic lids in favor of foil saved so much energy, water, and materials that it grew the bottom line by $1 million. "Waste is nothing less than incontrovertible evidence of inefficiency," Hirshberg preaches. "It's self-evident: When you become more efficient, you save money."

By enlisting his customers to join his crusade, Hirshberg has achieved an impressive measure of success: Stonyfield Farm is a model of sustainable business that others are increasingly imitating. Two juxtaposed facts neatly sum up Hirshberg's achievement: Stonyfield was the first company in the nation to offset 100 percent of its CO_2 emissions from its facility energy use. And more than a decade ago, Stonyfield not only became Kraft-like in its business reach, but also surpassed the food giant with U.S. yogurt sales that left its Breyers brand far behind. That is a testament to the power of customer engagement that Hirshberg has taken all the way to the bank.

RULES OF ENGAGEMENT

▶ *Make sure your customers are true believers.* The key to engaging your customers with a cause is to find people who identify with your mission and will happily pay a premium for the emotional connection they get from supporting it. Hirshberg started by looking for people with a concern for healthy eating, and he found them by letting masses of consumers sample his yogurt, who then passed on its virtues to their friends.

As customer engagement deepened, Stonyfield reinforced the emotional link to its customers by positioning itself as a fighter for a broader-based environmental cause. For example, Hirshberg's unconventional marketing in Chicago and Houston made commuters feel good about helping to minimize pollution; he then linked their self-satisfaction with the good taste of Stonyfield yogurt.

THE KEY TO ENGAGING YOUR CUSTOMERS WITH A CAUSE IS TO FIND PEOPLE WHO IDENTIFY WITH YOUR MISSION AND WILL HAPPILY PAY A PREMIUM FOR THE EMOTIONAL CONNECTION THEY GET FROM SUPPORTING IT.

▶ *Don't hesitate to break the rules.* If you are basing your relationship with customers on a cause, you are betting that you can make a profit on it even when the odds seem stacked against you. To succeed in such circumstances, you have to do whatever is needed to carry out your mission, even if it runs counter to common sense and conventional wisdom.

Hirshberg often broke standard business rules to do things that were counterintuitive. Among other transgressions, he overpaid his suppliers, failed to use traditional paid advertising, diverted income to charity, invested in a costly less conventional waste-treatment system, and priced his yogurt well above the competition. To Hirshberg's own surprise, his unorthodox moves helped his bottom line instead of hurting it, as business wisdom would have dictated. He chanced failure but considered his cause to be worth the risk. If you don't feel that way about your mission, don't try to make it a critical part of your business.

▶ *Use every available technique to tell your story.* Constant education is the key to engaging customers with a cause, so you must reinforce your message repeatedly. Stonyfield makes brilliant use of the 300 million yogurt container lids it churns out every year to deliver its message, exhort the faithful, and even exert political power. In letting kids take a role and learn about the business and the cows behind it, the Stonyfield.com Web site is a model for reinforcing its message to customers and recruiting a new generation to the cause.

▶ *Combine your crusade with hands-on product experience.* A crusade is a valuable tool, but it's not enough by itself. Customers must experience your product and like it before you can hope to engage them with your cause. Don't look down on old techniques such as handing out samples on the street. I live in Boston, and it's the rare week that someone doesn't hand me a free product sample as I walk through Copley Square. Similar to any other consumer, I usually try whatever I'm given. Short of cash for traditional advertising, Hirshberg and Kaymen wisely turned to sampling as a way to get their yogurt into the hands (and mouths) of potential consumers. They were confident that true yogurt lovers would taste the difference immediately—and they were right. Product attachment must precede cause engagement.

A CRUSADE IS A VALUABLE TOOL, BUT IT'S NOT ENOUGH BY ITSELF. CUSTOMERS MUST EXPERIENCE YOUR PRODUCT AND LIKE IT BEFORE YOU CAN HOPE TO ENGAGE THEM WITH YOUR CAUSE.

▶ *Find multiple ways to embed your cause in the hearts and minds of your customers.* If you need to quickly lift product sales to a certain level, product packaging and traditional advertising might not be the answer. Hirshberg boosted sales in a hurry by cleverly tying the emotions of Chicago commuters to his product message espousing a clean and healthy environment. If your strategy for engaging customers is to mount a crusade, you must be creative in both how you get customers to sample your product and how you get them to hear and embrace the idea that drives your message.

▶ *Make sure your cause has broad appeal.* If you want to achieve scale in your business, your cause must be unquestionable and generally accepted by the contingent you wish to attract. You don't want to be fighting a political or social war while trying to build your business. There will always be people who argue about the harm we humans are inflicting on the environment, but a broad segment of the population generally accepts the need for more environmental respect. It was no accident that Hirshberg's product aligned so well with his larger crusade—yogurt comes from the Earth through a cow's digestive system.

IF YOU WANT TO ACHIEVE SCALE IN YOUR BUSINESS, YOUR CAUSE MUST BE UNQUESTIONABLE AND GENERALLY ACCEPTED BY THE CONTINGENT YOU WISH TO ATTRACT. YOU DON'T WANT TO BE FIGHTING A POLITICAL OR SOCIAL WAR WHILE TRYING TO BUILD YOUR BUSINESS.

▶ *Be completely true to your cause.* The risk of engaging customers through a crusade is that you accidentally—or purposely—drift from the cause. Customers who join a crusade are very observant, and they can quickly become

cynical and might question your authenticity if you
stray. Stonyfield is a particularly impressive example of a
winning crusade, largely because Hirshberg has remained
so focused on carrying out his core beliefs. Everything
the company does confirms its commitment to the
environment.

NETWORKING IS VITAL TO THE
BOSTON SEARCH GROUP, A FIRM
THAT SPECIALIZES IN FINDING
TALENTED EXECUTIVES FOR
HIGH-TECH START-UPS. UNTIL
RECENTLY, HOWEVER, EVERY
TIME CLARK WATERFALL, THE
GROUP'S COFOUNDER AND
MANAGING DIRECTOR, WANTED
TO LUNCH WITH A PROSPECT
OUTSIDE OF BOSTON, HE FACED
A DAUNTING CHALLENGE JUST
GETTING THERE.

CHAPTER 3
WHAT COULD BE MORE
INSPIRING THAN CONVENIENCE
WITH ECONOMY?

Waterfall commutes by train to downtown Boston from nearby Hopkinton, Massachusetts. But a lunch date in, say, Waltham, 10 miles away, forced him to take his car. "I'd have to fight traffic on the way in to my office in the city, park, get dinged for a full-day rate by the garage, head out to Waltham, head back to my office, get dinged again for the full-day rate, and then have to make my way home on the Pike (the Massachusetts Turnpike) during rush hour," he recalls. "It was just maddening." The company tried keeping a car downtown for its staff to use, but the cost of parking and a plague of dead batteries made that solution ineffective.

The sanity saver turned out to be the convenient and economical Zipcar, the leading car-sharing service in the world. These days, whenever Waterfall or his colleagues need a car, they simply go to www.zipcar.com to reserve one of hundreds of autos kept in the Boston area. Waterfall can get a car whenever he wants, 24/7, and he can choose from among 25 makes and models, ranging from a Mini Cooper to a BMW. Using a powerful data network, the reservation is transmitted to the chosen automobile's onboard computer.

To pick up the car, Waterfall walks two blocks or less from his office to where it is parked in a permanently reserved space. He waves his personal Zipcard across the car's windshield, alerting the computer that the authorized renter has arrived. The door unlocks, and he sees the ignition key dangling from the steering post. If a thief were to break in, the dangling key would be of no use because the car won't start unless the computer has authenticated the driver.

Zipcar estimates that each one of its vehicles replaces over 15 privately-owned vehicles. But its value proposition to customers goes far beyond conservation. Zipcar's service is convenient, easy to use, and speaks to the intelligence of its customers. It offers a layered set of benefits that keep its customers going to its website, **www.zipcar.com**, to reserve cars.

The beauty of the Zipcar community is that we're all different shapes, sizes, and colors. But if you're unsure if Zipcar is for you, we've put together some scenarios.

I take public transit, but need a car sometimes.
- Public transportation (and even cabs) can't always get you where need to go. With 180 miles included with every reservation, you can find out what's at the end of the line. See what's included ▸

I want to save money.
- Zipcar members report an average monthly savings of more than $500 compared to car ownership. Whether you're a car owner or a taxi taker, there are savings to go around. Find out how much you could save ▸

I don't want the hassle of owning a car.
- Maybe you're looking to shed a car, or maybe you're looking for a way to never have to own at all. Either way, Zipcars practically take care of themselves: they have parking spaces, plus cleaning and maintenance crews.

I want to do my part to take care of our planet.
- Zipcars are good for the planet and the wallet. Each Zipcar takes 15-20 personally owned vehicles off the road. See why Zipcar is a sustainable transportation solution ▸

Once in a while I need a second car.
- Did your spouse or roommate take your car for the day? Hello, Zipcar. Thinking of adding another car to the family? First check out how much you could save by using Zipcar instead. Learn more ▸

I need a big car for a big job.
- Reserving Zipcars online (in seconds) beats the heck out of renting a moving truck, or bothering your brother-in-law for his pick up – reserve your own. Find cars (and trucks!) ▸

I want a cute car to match my new shoes.
- There's a Zipcar for every moment (and outfit). Go ahead and try them all.

I want to impress my boss.
- We have a couple of solutions: take them out in a swanky BMW, or save your company hundreds and hassles by joining Zipcar for Business. We see a promotion in your future. Learn about Zipcar for Business ▸

We try not to typecast anyone. So even if you don't see yourself here, Zipcar might still be for you. Convenience and savings seem to work for almost everybody. Otherwise, tell a friend.

Waterfall drives to his lunch meeting and back, parks the car in its customary spot, and returns to the office. He never has to worry about parking fees, maintenance, or car insurance. His monthly bill doesn't even include an extra fee for the gasoline he uses—it's included in the rate. If the tank needs filling, Waterfall uses the Zipcar credit card kept in the car's glove compartment. Using a Zipcar, the company boasts, "is as easy as getting cash from an ATM."

In a world increasingly beset by hassles, Zipcar's quick, simple convenience for business and personal use is a road map for success. More and more people are willing to pay a premium for genuine ease of use, as the expanding car-sharing field attests. But Zipcar leads the field because it is engaging with customers by delivering convenience that actually saves them money. The 65 percent or more of Zipcar users who decide against buying a car in the first place, or who end up selling the cars they had, save an average of $500 a month compared to car owners—and they can still drive whenever and wherever they want.

Zipcar has more than a quarter million card-carrying members, or Zipsters, and 5,000 automobiles in 13 major urban markets, including Boston, Toronto, New York, Philadelphia, San Francisco, and Washington, DC. It also has a European foothold in London. Since its merger in 2007 with Flexcar, it towers over the other 30 U.S. competitors in the car-sharing field. Zipcar's basic appeal is this: For an hourly charge of approximately $10, members can easily get a car when they need it without having to deal with the problems of automobile ownership. Zipcar, in effect, gives harried people more time to pursue their interests.

As a Zipcar advertisement jokingly puts it, "350 hours a year having sex. 420 looking for parking. What's wrong with this picture?"

Sharing car ownership works best for city dwellers who need a car for only a few hours and can put it back where they found it, making it available for other members to use. For a car-sharing company, the challenge is having enough, but not too many, cars in a given area. A company needs enough cars so that any member can find one at any time and without too much of a walk.

The car-sharing concept is at least two decades old in Europe. After seeing it in action in Berlin in 1999, Robin Chase, Zipcar's founder and original chief executive, had the light-bulb moment that produced the company. However, the idea has been a hard sell in the United States because Americans identify so strongly and personally with their vehicles—even though most cars are driven only about an hour a day and sit idle the rest of the time, piling up parking fees, insurance payments, and maintenance bills.

However, rising costs are combining with growing environmental awareness to gradually persuade more Americans to share the benefits and the drawbacks of owning cars. These days, thanks to its high-tech systems, Zipcar can keep each of its cars on the road for several hours a day, and any member needing an automobile can find one within a ten-minute walk. Car-sharing companies are proliferating, and major rental companies—including Enterprise, Hertz, and U-Haul—began testing the concept.

Every Zipcar replaces 15–20 privately owned vehicles, so it's no surprise that cities clogged with traffic and hard-pressed for parking space are delighted to cooperate with Zipcar and its rivals. Some cities even subsidize car sharing. The suburban cities of Alexandria and Arlington, Virginia, just outside Washington DC, offered a program to pay the membership fees for residents who want to join a car-sharing plan. Greenridge House, a senior citizens' home in Maryland, reimburses residents for their use of Zipcar.

Shared cars are a natural solution for any large organization in densely populated areas where parking is hard to come by. Zipcar has partnerships with major corporations and with more than 120 universities, including Wellesley outside of Boston, that have made cars available to students. In New York City, the Stuyvesant Town and Peter Cooper Village housing complexes offer Zipcar service to tenants. And Washington, DC, Metro transit officials have spurred subway use by placing Zipcars at dozens of Metro stations in the city and its suburbs; customers can take the subway most of the way to their destinations and finish their journeys by car. "We're part of the public transit fabric," notes Matthew Malloy, Zipcar's marketing vice president.

Founded in 2000 in Cambridge, Massachusetts, Zipcar quickly covered metropolitan Boston and spread to New York and Washington, DC. But buying all those cars soaked up a lot of capital, causing the company to sputter in 2003 when it ran out of funds for expansion. Zipcar's financial backers responded by installing Scott Griffith as CEO. Griffith is an engineer and former management consultant who, before taking the Zipcar post, headed software-maker Digital Goods.

Griffith told me he took the job because he was fascinated by the Zipcar concept and thought it had the potential to grow to millions of members worldwide. But he saw the need for a new business model that would engage people so thoroughly that it would change their lifestyles. "If you can optimize the model," he explains, "then the sky's the limit."

To achieve Zipcar's potential, Griffith decided to jettison the "heavy iron" of the company's old approach in favor of a more distributive, self-service model. He knew the changeover would not be easy: "We were actually asking people to change their basic attitude and behavior toward cars." But if the company could entice customers to try Zipcars for their convenience and then persuade them to embrace the concept wholeheartedly, Zipcar would move into the fast lane.

And that's just what happened. From only 150 cars and 4,000 customers when Griffith arrived in 2003, the company now has 35 times more cars and 65 times more customers. Sales and members have doubled each year, and some cities have been in the black since July 2004.

From my point of view, the most impressive and instructive Zipcar statistic is the number of full-time employees: It takes just 250 people to keep this fast-growing enterprise rolling. That's largely because Griffith's self-service model enlists members to do much of the work typically expected of staffers, from making their own reservations to filling their cars' gas tanks. Zipcar relies on members to report problems with cars, and members agree to abide by Zipcar's six simple rules: report damage, keep it clean, no smoking, fill 'er up, return on time, and keep pets in carriers.

Zipcar strives to simplify the work members are required to do, and technology eases the way. A user-friendly Web site enables a member to reserve a car without talking to a person; the reservation travels directly from the member to the car's onboard computer. A voice-mail system allows members to leave a message when reporting a problem; a distressed customer goes to the top of the list. The visor organizer holds fuel credit cards, making it simple for members to stop and refuel if needed.

LOOKING FOR ANSWERS

Zipcar has grown, in large measure, because of the drive and dedication of its chief executive. Before joining Zipcar, Griffith was stricken with cancer, a battle that changed his approach to life. "I was making a lot of money," he explains, "but I didn't like what I was doing at all. So I made a promise to myself that I was never again going to get into a situation where I wasn't passionate about my work." Zipcar's concept and potential fired his passion, and it shows.

When Griffith took over, Zipcar had only one vehicle parked in each of its various locations, which made potential customers nervous: "What if another Zipster wants to use the car at the same time I do?" they wondered. The company's less-than-popular answer was to go to a Zipcar parked farther away. Instead of engaging with the customer, the company's solution seemed to break its basic promise of convenience and was hardly calculated to increase the customer base. Yet the company was wary of buying more cars than it had to, and rightly so. How could Griffith untangle this knotty problem?

Zipcar had just entered the New York market that spring. "It was the right time of year, the high season," Griffith remembers. "Especially in the Northeast, people sort of shake off the winter blues and want to get out and drive." But Zipcar was choking in its new territory. Reluctantly, he approved a long-planned major advertising campaign to spread the word around the Big Apple. By midsummer, the results were in, and they were disappointing. The campaign had indeed introduced Zipcars to New Yorkers, and many of them had contacted the company— but hardly anyone was signing up. Market research unearthed the reason: Similar to potential customers everywhere else, New Yorkers thought their nearest Zipcar location was just too far away. Zipcar now defines its target market in each city where it operates as anyone who can walk less than ten minutes to a Zipcar. Today, that is 13 million people.

Griffith's response was fast and bold: "Stop screwing around with putting two or three cars into a market. Blitz the place. Put 100 cars into some New York neighborhoods, and if that works, put in another hundred. We'll lose money at first, but we'll learn what the number is where we'll start to make money." At the same time, in pursuit of a better way to engage with potential customers, he pushed his marketers to find the right neighborhoods—those with demographics that matched Zipcar's promise.

The model customer, it turned out, was relatively young, well educated, an early adopter of new technology, and committed to living in the city. By the end of the year, the Zipcar blitz was underway, aimed at zip codes with a high percentage of residents who fit that description. Instead of parking just one car in a certain area, Zipcar would have four or five. Instead of a dozen cars sprinkled throughout a zip code territory, Zipcar would have scores or maybe even hundreds. And it all worked incredibly well. Targeted customers were signing up in droves when they weren't busy telling their friends how easy it was to use Zipcar and how much money they were saving.

Griffith also upgraded the company's somewhat austere menu of cars. Prior to Griffith joining the company, the fleet mostly consisted of Volkswagen Beetles and Honda Civics. Today members can reserve what Zipcar calls "mood cars," including Mini Coopers, Prius hybrids, Mazda Miata convertibles, and even BMWs—more than 25 models in all. And if customers don't want to be branded as a renter, they can get a Zipcar without the big, lime-green "Z" on the door. However, most members don't care about that; if anything, they're proud to drive Zipcars. Corporate customers, who now make up 20 percent of Zipcar members, relish the range of choices and so do everyday drivers. The Civics and Golfs were "okay," says Christina Michaud, a teacher at Boston University who joined Zipcar three years ago, "but who wants to rent a Civic to go for a fun drive?" Michaud says the Mini Cooper is "the only car I feel I can actually park. And it's so fun. I feel happy and friendly in it."

Therefore, Zipcar's engagement with its customers was strengthened by giving them more: more nearby locations and more car choices to indulge their fantasies. Now not only does a member get a car when and where it's needed, but the company also guarantees to deliver "the car you want."

Griffith has also increased the company's engagement with customers by making their transactions simpler and more transparent. When he joined Zipcar, it charged low hourly rates plus mileage, the common car-sharing practice. But after spending time interviewing members when they returned their Zipcars to the parking areas, he decided to make some changes. "People loved us at $4 an hour, 45¢ a mile," he told me. "Then they'd use a car for a few hours, expecting a $15 bill, and it would be $35. Sticker shock." What the company needed was a way of simplifying the charges so that members could know in advance just what a trip would cost them.

Simplified pricing means that members now pay an hourly charge that includes 180 miles per day; anything over the limit costs drivers a standard 40-45 cents per mile. "If you give them too many miles," Griffith says, "they'll run the wheels off those cars, and they'll depreciate too fast." He also found a way to reward frequent users: Those who pre-commit to certain amounts of driving receive 15-20 percent discounts on standard hourly and daily rates.

To correct the imbalance created by cars being used mainly in the evening and on weekends, Griffith targeted businesspeople who primarily need cars on weekdays. He engaged with employees of large and small companies alike, but entrepreneurs and consultant types such as Waterfall have found car sharing particularly useful. Elan Ackerman, a special-events marketer in Manhattan, spends about $150 a month on Zipcars that he uses to pick up disc jockeys at the airport and to deliver cases of beer for his biggest client. He values the extra convenience Zipcar gives him for a lot less money and hassle than other options might demand. For example, if he had a company car, Ackerman says he would have to worry about capital costs, depreciation, maintenance, and insurance—and he would be spending $400 a month in parking fees alone.

Griffith has made the leap from engaging with corporate customers to finding corporate partners with little trouble. When a company's brand and demographics match those of Zipcar, he offers a co-branding arrangement. For example, IKEA sponsored 14 cars bearing both IKEA and Zipcar logos in Boston. IKEA then created "Zipcar parking only" spaces at its new store to entice Metro Boston residents to leave the city and visit its out-of-town location. The co-branded cars were available to Zipcar members at a discount that was reimbursed to Zipcar by IKEA.

Zipcar's corporate connections—Zipcar for Business (Z4B)— have paid off in a big way. In addition to adding hours to the average Zipcar's weekly use, Z4B now accounts for about 20 percent of all revenue.

With new learning from the launch in New York, Griffith revamped his marketing approach. By aiming his efforts directly at the targeted customers—what he calls "zone marketing"—he generally engages with more customers at far less cost.

Zipcar's customers tend to be young, well educated, technologically sophisticated city dwellers who cluster in characteristic neighborhoods. Similar to an army planning an invasion, Griffith and his marketers studied the maps of each Zipcar city, using postal codes and census data to find zones rich in drivers who fit the desired demographic. Then instead of paying a hefty price for blanket newspaper or TV ads, the Zipcar team focused on the people it wanted to reach.

They put up Zipcar posters in local theaters and left brochures in racks at restaurants. Employees set up booths at street fairs and gave Zipcar materials to residents exiting the subway or other mass-transit operations. In some zones, Zipcar workers parked outside Whole Foods stores, offering shoppers a free ride to their homes. Zipcar became impossible to ignore in its target neighborhoods.

The company's constantly evolving zone-marketing strategy, with its detailed matching of targeted customers and available cars, is a major competitive advantage, Griffith thinks. "I got goose bumps," he says, when he first saw the breakdown of all the zones in Boston and the way available cars dovetailed with the targeted customers. The CEO boasts that the strategy puts Zipcar on par with the patriots in the Revolutionary War—the Americans shot from behind trees while the British soldiers marched in tight formation out in the open, turning them into sitting ducks. Armed with zone-marketing weaponry, Griffith says that his Zipcar troops are "behind the trees," making it a lot easier to mow down the competition.

RULES OF ENGAGEMENT

▶ *Go beyond convenience with layered benefits.* Although
a strategy of convenience might be appealing, it might
not be enough to secure your customers and keep them
engaged. Customers are fickle and always want more.
But convenience becomes a powerful proposition when
combined with economy. Zipcar saw the benefits of
car-sharing for urban Americans, and it provided an
economical solution to problems ranging from the high
cost of ownership to the aggravation of traffic congestion
and the danger of environmental damage.

Then Zipcar extended its engagement proposition even
further, adding more choices and styles, and sending
the message to customers that they didn't need to
compromise: "You, too, can have a 'Beemer' to zip around
in on the weekend, or you can choose a VW to visit a
client." There is also a subtle appeal to being a member
of a community—a cadre of smart, with-it urbanites who
avoid the hassles of automobile ownership and share a
respect for the environment. It all adds up to a layered set
of benefits that continue to engage the customer.

▶ *Know what convenience means to your customers.* An
engagement strategy of convenience requires a deep
understanding of how your product or service will fill
a customer need. And what works for one group of
customers might not work for another. You might need
to use market segmentation, which Zipcar achieved with
its zone marketing. And if you are borrowing something
already in use elsewhere, make sure you adapt it to fit the

realities of your own market. Zipcar's founders knew going in that American customers would want 24/7 service and wouldn't walk as far as Europeans do to pick up their cars.

AN ENGAGEMENT STRATEGY OF CONVENIENCE REQUIRES A DEEP UNDERSTANDING OF HOW YOUR PRODUCT OR SERVICE WILL FILL A CUSTOMER NEED. AND WHAT WORKS FOR ONE GROUP OF CUSTOMERS MIGHT NOT WORK FOR ANOTHER.

▶ *Push your product or service proposition as far and as fast as you can.* Incrementalism doesn't work when using convenience and economy to engage your customers. Zipcar built the most advanced technology in the car-sharing field to enable customers to reserve a car, locate it, unlock it, and drive it away without any hassles. Customers don't worry about insurance, maintenance, depreciation, or parking fees; even gasoline is paid for with the Zipcar credit card. The cars are equipped with XM satellite radios and a voice-mail system to report problems. And a simplified pricing structure makes it easy to gauge the cost of using a car before you drive away.

INCREMENTALISM DOESN'T WORK WHEN USING CONVENIENCE AND ECONOMY TO ENGAGE YOUR CUSTOMERS.

▶ *Economy shouldn't mean no choice.* Customers always want to pay less while wanting more. Zipcar manages to deliver convenience for less, but it has also learned how to deliver more choice. Customers can choose from more than 25 car models to rent by the day or the hour. Separate plans are available for frequent users and occasional customers. The key to achieving real economy is to have a very efficient delivery model. Just look at how few people run the Zipcar business, and how much work Zipcar customers gladly do themselves. A very efficient business model also helps you direct money to where it counts— such as convenience and choice.

▶ *Identify your potential customers and find a way to tell them what you can do for them.* For Zipcar, this effort began with a demographic study of neighborhoods and expanded to concentrate on reaching customers where they lived—not by scattershot advertising, but with targeted brochures, posters, handouts, and individual marketing efforts. This kind of guerrilla marketing has helped many small companies to succeed and prosper.

▶ *Broaden the use of your product or service by engaging with new customers who don't overlap your current market.* A proposition that has great appeal and sustainability can find its way into multiple markets. Zipcar's cultivation of corporate members attracted much-needed weekday customers who put the cars to use for more hours each day without cutting into individual member use at night and on weekends.

▶ *Look for natural allies who will benefit from your success or who can use your product or service for their own benefit.* Going to market with a good business partner that shares your interest can accelerate growth. City governments saw the potential that Zipcar offered to ease congestion and parking problems, so cities have made it easier for the company to operate. Meanwhile, more than 120 college campuses, clogged by students' cars, have welcomed Zipcar service as an alternative to adding costly new parking spaces. And, through a partnership, IKEA subsidized a 30 percent discount on its co-branded Zipcars to reward customers and make it easier for them to visit IKEA stores. But you need to take the initiative. None of these natural allies leapt to Zipcar's aid until Zipcar showed them how they could profit from the alliance. And always be sure that you have selected allies whose business or societal interests are aligned with yours.

GOING TO MARKET WITH A GOOD BUSINESS PARTNER THAT SHARES YOUR INTEREST CAN ACCELERATE GROWTH.

EARLY IN 2004, MEMBERHEALTH WAS A NICE, LITTLE COMPANY HELPING SENIORS GET DISCOUNTS ON THEIR PRESCRIPTION DRUGS. CEO CHARLES HALLBERG PRESIDED OVER 20 EMPLOYEES IN A NONDESCRIPT OFFICE BUILDING NEAR CLEVELAND, OHIO, AND REVENUES FOR THAT YEAR TOPPED $6 MILLION. BUT THAT WAS BEFORE HALLBERG'S BRAINSTORM. ONLY THREE YEARS LATER, MEMBERHEALTH WAS THE FASTEST-GROWING COMPANY IN THE UNITED STATES, ACCORDING TO *INC.* MAGAZINE. ITS REVENUES HAD SOARED TO $1.24 BILLION, AND ITS THREE-YEAR GROWTH RATE WAS A MIND-BOGGLING 20,129.9 PERCENT. (I LOVE THAT LAST NINE-TENTHS OF A POINT. TALK ABOUT PRECISION.)

CHAPTER 4

WHAT COULD BE MORE INSPIRING THAN A TRUSTED CHANNEL?

How did Hallberg do it? By jumping aboard the Medicare Part D prescription drug bandwagon alongside some of the biggest insurers in the country—and then outperforming them by finding a better, more trusted channel for engaging with his company's customers. The key to Hallberg's outsized success was his decision to join with the nation's mom-and-pop pharmacies to sign up Medicare patients for the drug program. The pharmacists make the seniors happy by lowering their costs, counseling them about their healthcare, and making sure their medicines don't interact in dangerous ways. Now MemberHealth's Community CCRx plan is the country's fourth-largest Part D plan, with 63,000 pharmacies serving 1.2 million members. It is also ranked number one in the nation in customer satisfaction, based on a recent government-sponsored survey.

Living in Boston, I had no idea that about 24,000 independent pharmacies were still in business across America. In large, urban communities, the big chains—CVS, Walgreens, Duane Reade, Rite Aid, and the like—dominate the market. But as I learned in talking with Hallberg, independent pharmacies are still alive and well in the vast majority of the country.

Like his competitors, Hallberg still had to stay within the rigid rules of the Part D program, which Congress set up as part of the Medicare Modernization Act of 2003. But unlike his rivals, he managed to "align the interests of all the players" in the game; he told me: Medicare patients get better care and lower costs, the pharmacists get a good deal and the professional satisfaction of playing a real role in patient care, the government saves money on the cost of the program, and

You can see from its website, **www.mhrx.com**, how MemberHealth appeals to all its constituencites: the customer (individuals), brokers & consultants, employers & groups, and pharmacists. It actively engages all its channels.

MemberHealth racks up phenomenal growth and a handsome profit, too.

For Hallberg, the alliance with the pharmacists was a natural move. As a young lawyer in the 1970s, he worked for the Revco pharmacy chain and soaked up its corporate culture. "Revco was a pioneer in discounting," he says, "and its focus was on delivering service, quality, and price savings every day. That's the same concept we use at MemberHealth."

After a stint as vice president of a prescription benefit management company (PBM), Hallberg founded his own PBM in 1991, negotiating with pharmacies and drug manufacturers to get discounts for his members and corporate healthcare plans. The day after this company was sold in 1998, Hallberg started MemberHealth. With a $75,000 loan and an office in his basement, he built it into a solid business with 13 employees. Unlike his competitors, Hallberg explains, he passed on to his members the entire discount he negotiated with the drug industry. That was "relatively unknown methodology at the time," he says dryly; other PBMs pocketed part of the savings.

His first big break came in 2002, when Ohio decided to offer its senior citizens a state-sponsored discount-drug plan. Hallberg's little company made a bid for the contract and beat out several billion-dollar rivals. Certainly, MemberHealth's reputation for treating its customers well helped it land the contract, but the key factor was this innovation: Hallberg proposed to give seniors a single membership card, the Golden Buckeye Card, that would be good for discounts on drugs from any manufacturer who agreed to participate.

At the time, many drug makers offered discount cards for low-income patients, but only for use on the card giver's drugs. "Mabel might be on five medications from three different drug manufacturers," Hallberg says, "but they have three completely different programs. For antitrust reasons, they can't talk to each other." The discount varied with each card, too, and some were good only on certain days of the week. Not surprisingly, many seniors were confused. It was up to the pharmacist to sort out which card applied to which drug. MemberHealth's Golden Buckeye Card bundled all the discounts into one card. Hallberg likens it to a bank card: "You can use it at any ATM, and the computers will figure it out at the end of the day." (Similar to the Zipcar case in the previous chapter, MemberHealth's engagement strategy has strong components of convenience.)

Pharmacists loved the Ohio plan's less-confusing and more-efficient arrangement, and so did the seniors. MemberHealth signed up 2 million members and expanded its staff to 20 people. It was still tiny compared to giant insurers such as Humana and UnitedHealthcare, but its Golden Buckeye success had emboldened Hallberg. When Congress voted in favor of the Part D drug program covering 40 million Medicare patients, he decided to bid again.

Early in 2004, when the federal Centers for Medicare and Medicaid Services (CMS) held a meeting in Baltimore to explain the rules for Part D, some 5,000 would-be plan directors showed up or joined by phone hoping for a piece of the action. Hallberg and his staff members ran into people they knew from Computer Sciences Corporation (CSC), a $15 billion technology giant with a proven track record as a federal contractor (and my previous employer). "We'd never partnered with the federal government, and they'd never done any drug programs," Hallberg recalls. "It was a great marriage. (CSC was) awarded a contract for the first phase, and we were their subcontractor."

The first phase of Part D involved a straightforward discount card that was to be used for 18 months before the full-scale drug insurance plan went into effect. "It was a marvelous idea," Hallberg told me, "because it made a level playing field that allowed companies like ours to get into the game." The two-phase structure also gave companies time to plan and gather staff to handle the huge new business they would take on in Phase II.

MemberHealth seized on the Medicare discount card to begin its partnership with the nation's pharmacists, building on the relationship it had begun in Ohio with the Golden Buckeye Card. Hallberg's earlier positive experience partnering with pharmacists led him to approach the National Community Pharmacists Association (NCPA), the trade group representing mainly mom-and-pop drugstores and small chains. The large chains, which were members of the National Association of Chain Drug Stores (NACDS), had already joined up with the mail-order discounter Express Scripts to administer their discount programs, and they wanted the NCPA to come under their tent. Hallberg, however, had other plans.

"I begged Bruce Roberts, the executive vice president of NCPA, to meet with me and my colleague from CSC," Hallberg explains. "He was very polite, but, frankly, I wasn't getting very good results. But after about the 18th phone call, he said,

'I'll give you 20 minutes over my lunch hour.'" That was enough. "We literally had a handshake that afternoon," Hallberg recalls. "We went in, made a presentation, talked about our approach to the market, and Bruce stuck his neck out and agreed with us."

Hallberg attributes his success to his understanding of the people who work in the retail pharmacy industry. He knew they wanted respect and a professional role in healthcare. State regulators require pharmacists to have advanced degrees, he reminded me, and they come out of school as sophisticated clinicians with a wealth of knowledge. Then they find a job and discover themselves being instructed, as Hallberg put it, to "count 30 pills and put them in the bottle, and let the computer do the rest." Hallberg says, "They were being sidelined and marginalized. Part of our promise was, 'We will deal you into the healthcare equation,' and we've continued to do that."

With the NCPA's backing, Hallberg was able to enlist small-market pharmacists to help enroll seniors in the discount plan. That was particularly advantageous in little towns and rural communities where pharmacists are trusted healthcare consultants. The pharmacists were a great help, too, in assuaging the doubt and apprehension hanging over the whole Part D program. The media were full of foreboding about how seniors would cope with the complex new plans. "If you remember," Hallberg says, "there was a concern whether anybody would show up and play. Everyone was hugely skeptical about the likelihood of success." But it was natural and easy for people to ask their pharmacists for advice, and although the pharmacists were forbidden to favor any one plan, nothing could stop them from handing out applications and explaining how the individual plans would work.

Unlike some large rivals that printed millions of application forms and lost money in the process, MemberHealth controlled costs by mailing out small batches of applications to the pharmacists and sending more only as needed. "We enrolled 450,000 people," Hallberg says, "and our discount-drug program was profitable. Not everyone's was."

Phase II of the Part D program augured a major role change for both MemberHealth and CSC. As discounters, they were still functioning as hired benefit managers and working on a cost-plus basis. In Phase II, they became insurers, taking on the risk that the members' monthly premiums and the government's payments for drugs might not cover their costs. "As a PBM, you don't have any skin in the game," Hallberg explains. "You're basically adding a fee to every pharmacy prescription. As an insurance company, our skin is in the game; we are at risk. So if we do a good job, we'll make money. If we do a poor job, we'll lose our shirt." And at the last minute, literally on the day their bid was to be submitted to the CMS, CSC decided that health insurance wasn't its game. It would continue to supply technology if MemberHealth got the contract, but CSC's managers didn't want to take the lead.

"The thought that went through my head was, 'Yahoo!'" says Hallberg. "We were mentally and intellectually ready to step into that role. But there was no time for high-fives." His crew had to scramble to delete "CSC" wherever it appeared and substitute "MemberHealth" on several hundred pages of documents. It took all afternoon, and when they finally sped off in a car to hand-deliver the application to CMS, they were dangerously close to the 5 p.m. deadline. Leafing through the papers on the way, a staff member found one more place where "MemberHealth" had to be substituted for "CSC." When no one in the car could produce a pen, she whipped out her mascara wand, crossed out CSC, and wrote in MemberHealth. The bid was submitted on time, mascara smudges and all.

MemberHealth was chosen as one of ten national contractors for Part D in a field of formidable competitors. For example, the AARP endorsed giant UnitedHealthcare, which was running a national ad campaign and television commercials. Hallberg had no marketing or advertising budget, just his plan and the pharmacists handing out brochures and applications. The guidelines prevented the pharmacists from becoming advocates, Hallberg told me: "There are very strict rules about what they can say and do, and we are rigorous about educating the pharmacists not to cross that line." When new members were ready to sign up, CCRx agents went into stores to accept the applications. Nevertheless, Hallberg says that, without a doubt, the pharmacists helped.

THE SECRET (OR NOT-SO-SECRET) RECIPE FOR SUCCESS

The "secret sauce" of the MemberHealth plan's success, Hallberg told me, is his insistence on pleasing all parties involved in the transaction—the most important being the customer. "It is always about the beneficiary," he says. "The retail pharmacy relies on that beneficiary coming into the store every month to buy drugs. We could have a wonderful pharmacy-centric system, but if we didn't, first and foremost, start with the beneficiary, we'd never get to that second step."

Hallberg deserves kudos. His customers are evidently happy with the plan: In a 2007 survey of 4,500 Part D members conducted by Wilson Health Information, CCRx ranked first in customer satisfaction.

The plan now fills 60 million prescriptions a year, serving nearly 7 percent of all the people enrolled in Part D plans. More telling still is what his customers say to others. And whatever it is, it must be powerful because 60 percent of MemberHealth's new business comes through word-of-mouth referrals from existing customers.

Although CCRx isn't the cheapest plan in terms of monthly membership fees, its basic service is near the bottom of the price scale in most states. What the beneficiaries want, Hallberg explains, is "someone of authority to help them sort through complex issues. They don't necessarily need to know that this is the cheapest or the best. They want to know, 'Is this okay? Is this good for me? Am I okay with this one?' They want the comfort."

At MemberHealth, that comfort begins with its formulary, the list of drugs that qualify for discounts. To guarantee the formulary's fairness and objectivity, the company farmed it out to an independent group of experts at a prestigious pharmacy school. Their mandate, Hallberg says, was to "forget the manufacturers. Build us a formulary that is the purest, most clinically appropriate." The result was a list that included 98 percent of all the drugs on the Medicare master list, thus assuring members that it had been compiled for their benefit, not the Big Pharmaceuticals'. Companies whose drugs were excluded had the option of coming back to MemberHealth to negotiate supply of those medications at a lower cost.

All new members of the CCRx plan are given a "Welcome Review," which consists of a one-on-one consultation with a pharmacist to explain how the plan works, review their medications and make sure drug combinations don't cause dangerous reactions, and look for generics that can substitute for more expensive brand-name drugs. Unlike most plans, CCRx dispenses generics free to its members. MemberHealth says 66 percent of its prescriptions are filled with generic drugs, among the highest percentages of any Part D plan. In the first year of the program, CCRx members saved themselves $1.1 million a month by switching to generic prescriptions.

As for the pharmacists who serve the CCRx plan members, they get the satisfaction of providing actual care to their customers. What is more, they are freed from the chore of charging copayments for generic drugs that, in most cases, amount to little more than a dollar per prescription. To make up for the revenue lost in switching away from expensive brand-name drugs, MemberHealth pays pharmacists a larger dispensing fee for generic prescriptions than the dispensing fee for the brand drugs. Additionally, MemberHealth pays quarterly bonuses if they increase their percentage of generic prescriptions. Pharmacists also benefit from the fact that, unlike most of its competitors, MemberHealth doesn't offer a cut-rate mail-order service that steals business from local pharmacies. And CCRx's success even engaged the big drugstore chains; now these chains are joining up with MemberHealth and its mom-and-pop pharmacies.

The government is the third party in Part D transactions, and it, too, benefits from the CCRx plan. On average, generic drugs cost just 20 percent as much as brand names, so every prescription switched to a generic saves the taxpayers money. Over time, Hallberg says, MemberHealth's emphasis on using generic drugs will save the government tens, if not hundreds, of millions of dollars. "CMS loves our plan, big time," Hallberg told me—and no wonder.

As for MemberHealth, it's doing well by doing good. "I hate to say it, but we have built-in growth," Hallberg explains. "Every year, more people take more medications." That's to the general good, he argues, as new drugs prolong lives and keep people out of the hospital. But it's an inescapable fact of life that the longer people live, the more illness they will have and the more medicines they will need. "We're dealing with an infirm population," he told me. "They've all got something wrong." And CCRx helps make it better.

Hallberg owes his success primarily to the passage of the Medicare Modernization Act, he told me; it created the opportunity that MemberHealth could exploit. But Hallberg had a lot of competition, and he bested those rivals because he had a valuable store of knowledge that he used to create advantage, a sound business plan, and great execution. "We really knew our content and our subject matter. We knew the market," he admits. "Second, we had a plan, and we knew how to execute on it. I knew we had the right approach with the retail pharmacy channel because I know those people."

At the beginning of Phase II, he says, "we told our investors that we would enroll a million people in the first year. They thought it would be a home run if we did maybe 600,000. They said, 'Wow, that would be out of the park.' And we did, in fact, enroll a million people. ...I have to say that my team (executed our plan), in my opinion, damn near flawlessly."

At this writing, MemberHealth is looking for expanded space in the Cleveland area to house a workforce that has grown to 160 employees and about 600 contract workers. The company also manages discounts for corporate health plans and retiree groups. And its pharmacist consultations are being expanded to more formal Medication Therapy Management services, which will emphasize prevention, wellness, and medications taken correctly. Hallberg is trying to establish the concept of a "primary-care pharmacist" who can help patients by making them healthier, heading off adverse drug interactions, and improving their lives.

MemberHealth's spectacular growth caught the attention of corporate suitors early on, and in 2007, Universal American Financial Corporation, a health- and life-insurance-holding company, acquired it for a dazzling $630 million. The combined company now serves more than 2.1 million people and has $5 billion in revenue. Hallberg is staying on as the CEO of the MemberHealth operation.

"We have fun here," he told me. "Not a goofy dot-com company sort of fun. It's serious stuff, but it's fun. Every day, we look at each other and realize we have 1,300,000 people whose lives we are helping. And we can do that and make money at the same time. Goodness gracious, how cool is that?"

RULES OF ENGAGEMENT

▶ *Know your customer and your channel partners.* Most companies spend a lot of time getting to know their customers. After all, that's the first rule of customer engagement. But most companies don't give enough thought to their market channels and channel partners, and how those partners can enhance a customer experience. Look for partners both you and your customers trust, as Hallberg did for MemberHealth.

MOST COMPANIES SPEND A LOT OF TIME GETTING TO KNOW THEIR CUSTOMERS. AFTER ALL, THAT'S THE FIRST RULE OF CUSTOMER ENGAGEMENT. BUT MOST COMPANIES DON'T GIVE ENOUGH THOUGHT TO THEIR MARKET CHANNELS AND CHANNEL PARTNERS, AND HOW THOSE PARTNERS CAN ENHANCE A CUSTOMER EXPERIENCE.

Not knowing your channel partners can diminish how your customers experience your product or service. Until recently, that was the case with automobile dealers. Buying a new car—or, worse, a used car—was always dicey. You gritted your teeth, ready to endure a bargaining session and hoping you would get what you were promised at the price you agreed to pay. But when Vehix and similar Internet services made the dealer cost of an automobile known to the world, dealers stopped haggling about price and started paying attention to service and customer experience. They became better channel partners for automobile manufacturers, and some customers now even like and trust them.

Hallberg knew and understood the added value local pharmacists could bring to his customers. He also knew that, in rural and suburban communities, a pharmacist is often the first person a customer turns to for healthcare help.

▶ *Help your channel partner deliver more to the customer.* You can choose to have a passive relationship with the distributors or sellers of your product, but if you can help them do their job better, they will work harder for you. Enabling pharmacists to provide generic drugs for free was a brilliant move. And MemberHealth also remained very intent on making sure that the pharmacists made sustainable profits.

But to help your partner deliver more, you also need to understand your partner's business model: How does a partner really operate and generate its profits? Sometimes a partner is reluctant to give you the degree of transparency needed to create an efficient and productive working partnership. But don't give up. Be transparent yourself and engage your partner at a new level of trust.

Hallberg already knew his partners' businesses very well. You might have to work harder to get to know yours.

▶ *The deal must contain something for everyone.* If your business model is based on the contributions of multiple players, each one must receive a substantive benefit to keep all the players in the game and doing their jobs. The MemberHealth business model includes customers (aka beneficiaries), pharmacists, the federal government, and MemberHealth itself. The beneficiaries conveniently get the drugs they need at a fair price—and sometimes even for free; they also get to do business with people they know and trust. The pharmacists do a good business at a fair profit, and the complexity of their transactions is reduced; they also get increased professional satisfaction. The government gets the cost benefits of an efficient service provider. And MemberHealth gets the benefit of a growing, profitable business. Everyone wins and contention is removed from the system of doing business. (Later in this book, I introduce a similar situation through a company called Right Media.)

IF YOUR BUSINESS MODEL IS BASED ON THE CONTRIBUTIONS OF MULTIPLE PLAYERS, EACH ONE MUST RECEIVE A SUBSTANTIVE BENEFIT TO KEEP ALL THE PLAYERS IN THE GAME AND DOING THEIR JOBS.

▶ *Keep your eye on the end customer.* When lots of people are involved in a business model, it's possible to get distracted and forget who the ultimate customer really is. I often see this in large corporations when people in departments and business functions start talking about "internal customers." I always remind people that the only real customer is the person who pays for a company's product or service. Although a business model must benefit all the players, it should be designed from the perspective of the ultimate customer. In the case of MemberHealth, the beneficiary is the ultimate customer.

I ALWAYS REMIND PEOPLE THAT THE ONLY REAL CUSTOMER IS THE PERSON WHO PAYS FOR A COMPANY'S PRODUCT OR SERVICE.

▶ *Layer on benefits to keep customers engaged.* A MemberHealth beneficiary is first engaged by the benefit of doing business with a trusted pharmacist. But then look at how MemberHealth has added additional benefits: low-cost drugs, convenience, and the elimination of complexity and multiple cards. Engaging customers should not be a static exercise. The more value you can deliver, the longer you will keep the customer engaged.

ENGAGING CUSTOMERS SHOULD NOT BE A STATIC EXERCISE. THE MORE VALUE YOU CAN DELIVER, THE LONGER YOU WILL KEEP THE CUSTOMER ENGAGED.

▶ *Consider giving something away for free.* For a profit-making company, this advice might seem counterintuitive, but look at how making generic drugs free worked for

MemberHealth. It encouraged the right choices and lowered everyone's costs. Giving something of value away for free might also encourage customers to do other business with you. And for MemberHealth, the free drugs are not just samples; they are part of an ongoing business proposition.

I recently attended a lecture by the musician and sage Jimmy Buffett. He drew a distinction between the music industry, which is made up of performers like himself, and the record industry. The latter, he argued, was in a state of breakdown because of its unwillingness to adapt to new realities and because it has lived off practices that have taken advantage of musicians for years.

A good deal of music is now available for free on the Internet, but rather than change its business model, the record industry's response has been to sue its customers to prevent them from taking advantage of the free access. Everyone knows that the Internet will eventually make music, as with most information, free or almost free, but the record industry is ignoring this reality. However, Buffett makes all his live concerts available for free so that people who might not be able to attend the performance can still hear his music. In the end, they buy CDs of other Buffett performances.

Just be sure that what you give away for free has real value to your customers. I promise that it will keep them engaged.

AFTER A GRUELING 10-DAY HUNT IN THE ARCTIC NATIONAL WILDLIFE REFUGE NOT LONG AGO, BOB PARSONS STILL HADN'T GOTTEN WHAT HE'D GONE TO ALASKA FOR: A GRIZZLY BEAR. RELUCTANT TO LEAVE EMPTY-HANDED, THE PIONEERING INTERNET ENTREPRENEUR CONVINCED HIS GUIDE NOT TO DESERT HIM. THE GUIDE STAYED ON, AND PARSONS GOT HIS GRIZZLY THE NEXT DAY.

CHAPTER 5
WHAT COULD BE MORE INSPIRING THAN SIMPLIFYING COMPLEXITY?

Parsons doesn't give up easily, and he usually gets what he wants—be it a grizzly or a successful business.

In 1997, flush with cash after selling his first software company, he launched a company called Jomax Technologies. It floundered. Not yet ready to abandon his idea, Parsons gave the provider of Internet services a catchy new name, GoDaddy.com, and held on. Go Daddy was showing signs of new life when the dot-com crash sent it reeling. Worse yet, Parsons lost heavily in the stock market downturn. By early 2001, as he watched the ailing company eat up his remaining cash, Parsons knew that Go Daddy was going nowhere. What to do?

"I went to a resort in Hawaii to be by myself and make plans," he recalls. "One day I noticed that the guy parking my car was really happy doing his job." It occurred to Parsons that if he tried to keep Go Daddy going and failed, his life would not end. Maybe he'd park cars, but so what? He could still be happy.

Parsons returned to Go Daddy's headquarters in Scottsdale, Arizona, with new determination. In October 2001, cash flow turned positive. It was the beginning of the beginning. Soon Parsons was starring in his favorite role: the man a bad break can't defeat, whether he's stalking bears or starting companies.

For a guy with a never-give-up attitude, it might surprise you to learn that he's a true believer in making things simple for his customers—even if it means that he and his team have to manage extraordinary complexity behind the scenes. At Go Daddy, Parsons pares away the complexity with a business model that relies on the basics: Give customers feature-rich

BOB PARSONS' 16 RULES for SUCCESS
in business & life in general.

1 Get and stay out of your comfort zone.
I believe that not much happens of any significance when we're in our comfort zone. I hear people say, "But I'm concerned about security." My response to that is simple: "Security is for cadavers."

2 Never give up.
Almost nothing works the first time it's attempted. Just because what you're doing does not seem to be working, doesn't mean it won't work. It just means that it might not work the way you're doing it. If it was easy, everyone would be doing it, and you wouldn't have an opportunity.

3 When you're ready to quit, you're closer than you think.
There's an old Chinese saying that I just love, and I believe it is so true. It goes like this: "The temptation to quit will be greatest just before you are about to succeed."

4 With regard to whatever worries you, not only accept the worst thing that could happen, but make it a point to quantify what the worst thing could be.
Very seldom will the worst consequence be anywhere near as bad as a cloud of "undefined consequences." My father would tell me early on, when I was struggling and losing my shirt trying to get Parsons Technology going, "Well, Robert, if it doesn't work, they can't eat you."

5 Focus on what you want to have happen.
Remember that old saying, "As you think, so shall you be."

6 Take things a day at a time.
No matter how difficult your situation is, you can get through it if you don't look too far into the future, and focus on the present moment. You can get through anything one day at a time.

7 Always be moving forward.
Never stop investing. Never stop improving. Never stop doing something new. The moment you stop improving your organization, it starts to die. Make it your goal to be better each and every day, in some small way. Remember the Japanese concept of Kaizen. Small daily improvements eventually result in huge advantages.

8 Be quick to decide.
Remember what General George S. Patton said: "A good plan violently executed today is far and away better than a perfect plan tomorrow."

9 Measure everything of significance.
I swear this is true. Anything that is measured and watched, improves.

10 Anything that is not managed will deteriorate.
If you want to uncover problems you don't know about, take a few moments and look closely at the areas you haven't examined for a while. I guarantee you, problems will be there.

11 Pay attention to your competitors, but pay more attention to what you're doing.
When you look at your competitors, remember that everything looks perfect at a distance. Even the planet Earth, if you get far enough into space, looks like a peaceful place.

12 Never let anybody push you around.
In our society, with our laws and an even playing field, you have just as much right to what you're doing as anyone else, provided that what you're doing is legal.

13 Never expect life to be fair.
Life isn't fair. You make your own breaks. You'll be doing good if the only meaning "fair" has to you is something that you pay when you get on a bus (i.e., fare).

14 Solve your own problems.
You'll find that by coming up with your own solutions, you'll develop a competitive edge. Masura Ibuka, the co-founder of SONY,® said it best: "You never succeed in technology, business, or anything by following the others." There's also an old Asian saying that I remind myself of frequently. It goes like this: "A wise man keeps his own counsel."

15 Don't take yourself too seriously.
Lighten up. Often, at least half of what we accomplish is due to luck. None of us are in control as much as we like to think we are.

16 There's always a reason to smile.
Find it. After all, you're really lucky just to be alive. Life is short. More and more, I agree with my little brother. He always reminds me:

"We're not here for a long time, we're here for a GOOD TIME!"

www.bobparsons.com

Bob Parsons is not afraid to share his beliefs on the Go Daddy website, **www.GoDaddy.com**. You can see how his "tough guy" attitude—combined with buoyant optimism—got him through the challenges of building Go Daddy and sustaining its market position.

products, low pricing, and great support from real people located on-site and rigorously trained to solve any and every problem. And Go Daddy's customers just love it; they have steadily expanded the company's market share while lavishing the company with praise.

Hardly a Web site flickers onto your computer screen today without promising to make life easier—whether you're trying to buy a product, do business through the site, or access its Customer Care center—but few live up to the claim. Learning to navigate the typical site often takes hours, and Customer Care representatives can leave customers more confused than when they started. Not so at Go Daddy, where employees untangle the inherent complexities of helping customers register domain names and create Web sites, while also offering a varied palette of Internet-hosting services and e-business software.

Go Daddy isn't like most dot-com companies whose operations are a complicated maze of overlapping responsibilities and wasteful habits. Parsons has aimed his tech knowledge and laserlike focus on what really matters to the management of his company and its interface with customers. He maintains a flat organization, letting well-trained people make decisions without interference from complicating layers of management. The streamlined structure automatically eliminates much of the complexity, and Parsons' insistence on in-house product development and unwavering dedication to comprehensive customer support breaks down the rest.

The success of Parsons' formula is writ large in hard numbers. In little more than a decade, Go Daddy has attracted more than

6 million customers, registered more than 32 million domain
names, and built a worldwide market share of 46 percent
(impressive, considering there are more than 1,000 registrar
competitors). It's a performance worthy of an IndyCar racing
champion such as Danica Patrick, a comparison not lost on
Parsons and his Go Daddy marketing team—but more on that
later.

A DIRT ROAD LEADS TO RICHES

After selling Parsons Technology, his software company, in 1994,
the noncompete provisions in the sale agreement required
Parsons to retire for a year. He hated it. As soon as his time was
up, he told me, "I hired a few very sharp people, started a new
company, and got into the Internet stream." He had no vision,
no product, no business plan, and no model for engaging
customers—really. "Go Daddy was started with no ideas," says
the straight-talking Parsons. "I figured we'd just try this and that
and see what made money." He believed that he would find a
viable product faster from the inside than trying to speculate
about one from the outside. Everyone I know, including those
with deep pockets, does it the other way.

He called the company Jomax —after a dirt road. "The name
didn't matter. It didn't have to. At that point we weren't doing
anything." During the next few months, he built Web sites and
set up networks and tried out all sorts of ideas. "I learned that
it's a whole lot easier finding things that don't work than
things that do." Eventually, Parsons returned to his earliest
successes as a developer of intellectual properties software.

He created WebSite Tonight, a program to help organizations and individuals build their own sites. That called for a new company name. Someone suggested "Big Daddy," but it was taken. Then someone else, using the "Go" command on America Online, typed in "Go Daddy," and the domain name was available. "We bought it, just as a joke," Parsons says. "The next day we joked to everyone that it was going to be our new name. They laughed, but the name stuck."

While shopping his Web site builder program, Parsons began running into the arcane and complex world of domain name registrars. He was not impressed: "They were overpriced, service was horrific, and their systems were worse." He thought Go Daddy could do it better by attracting customers with low-price domain names and then selling them software to simplify site development. One year and a million dollars later, his system was in place and the Internet Corporation for Assigned Names and Numbers (ICANN) accredited Go Daddy as a *bona fide* domain name registrar. (ICANN is the not-for-profit global partnership that coordinates unique Internet identifiers.)

Go Daddy now registers or renews or transfers a domain name every second. It offers many other services, including Web site, blog, and iPod hosting; e-mail packages and account management; a secure e-commerce program to encrypt online transactions; and both do-it-yourself Web site design and a new customized service. The evolution of its product offerings has been accompanied by increasingly rapid corporate growth. Today the enterprise consists of six sites in three states employing more than 2,000 people, the vast majority of whom work at Go Daddy's Customer Care centers.

These employees are not just any old hired hands, but what Parsons lauds as "really psyched employees." They are psyched because he makes them that way by paying top dollar and offering extra incentives such as Harley-Davidson motorcycles, cars, and vacations (taxes included) in return for delivering the best customer support service in the business and a constant stream of new and improved products from a crack band of in-house innovators.

Try calling the big names of the tech world, and you're likely to meet frustration. You're lucky, Parsons points out, "if you can find somebody to talk to. You get transferred all over the place. You'll never get an answer. Your issues will never get satisfied." In contrast, a call to Go Daddy quickly connects you to a real live person who knows "exactly what you need to know and will handle your situation in spades," he says.

Parsons understands that when technological systems continually evolve and are not necessarily intuitive, "people have to be helped, and they need to have an organization that is going to communicate with them on a one-to-one basis." So Go Daddy does not outsource or offshore its customer support services. His team is on-site and on call 24 hours a day, seven days a week.

Parsons is also a true believer in "invented here." Most of Go Daddy's technology is developed and maintained in-house; nothing is licensed to or from outsiders. As a result, Go Daddy people know all products intimately and can serve customers intelligently. Its IT people are based in the United States, near the service support team members who answer the phones.

If a breakdown or problem occurs, the technology experts are right there to fix it.

Customers have only one telephone number to call and need to speak to just one person, because all Customer Care center employees are trained to handle any problem or customer inquiry—whether it's related to billing, design, repair, or anything in between. All needed help is free of charge. It's the ultimate example of simplifying a customer's life.

It's not only problems that set Go Daddy's Customer Care teams in motion. Salespeople are trained to make the engagement complete by calling every customer to say "thank you" and to answer any questions about a product within a week of its purchase. People don't forget that kind of service, Parsons says. Customers approach him in airports (he's easily recognizable from several photos on the Go Daddy site) and rave about the attention they get.

It's easy to see why Go Daddy's Customer Care teams turn a handsome profit when many of its competitors' operations throw off nothing but red ink.

Nevertheless, I wondered whether the average Customer Care representative could handle the really tough assignments—the ones from people with complex questions who often want to speak directly to the president of the company. No such problems arise at Go Daddy because Parsons has put together a "SWAT team made up of our very best Customer Care reps" to field the high-level questions. They are part of his so-called

Office of the President, and each carries the title Assistant to the President.

Besides handling the knottiest problems, these people perform another vital task: They issue a weekly report listing any new problems or new wrinkles in old ones—"opportunities," in Parsons' parlance. The report goes to management and the in-house product development group, which is expected to engineer fixes within a week, two at most. Its 200 members usually act fast because their incentive pay goes up when the number of complaints goes down.

Simplicity also extends to product development—after a product goes public, a team is assigned to it and never leaves. The arrangement eliminates the usual snafus that arise at other companies when teams move from project to project. Go Daddy developers become intensely familiar with everything about a product, including its problems. Good thing, too, because Parsons requires an update on every product every two weeks.

The rewards and incentives for staff members are the carrot part of what Parsons calls "a fiercely managed company." A firm believer in the define-measure-improve approach, he wields the stick by demanding a daily profit-and-loss statement for each division, every morning. The company has developed its own management information systems that show sales, for example, on an hourly basis along with previous performance.

But a well-managed company that makes great products backed up by equally great service can still flop if too few people know about it. So unlike Go Daddy competitors that you've never heard of, Parsons has opted to supplement typical Internet and word-of-mouth advertising with traditional television spots that appear during some of the nation's most watched events, such as the Super Bowl or IndyCar and NASCAR racing competitions.

Convinced that nondescript ads designed to please everyone are worthless, he doesn't flinch from edgy but humorous spots featuring people like race-car driver Danica Patrick and Go Daddy Girl Candice Michelle, a *Playboy* cover girl. The intent is to stand out from the crowd—and Go Daddy's ads do. "I'm very ready to alienate 10 to 15 percent of viewers to really get the attention of 85 to 90 percent," Parsons says. "You've got to make yourself known."

Still, he doesn't assume that his controversial spots will automatically sell products. Similar to everything else underlying Go Daddy's enormous success, marketing ploys, including every one of its 900 television ads per week, are measured: "We know within an hour or two if one or another worked," Parsons explains, "and if it didn't, we yank it."

Parsons' determination to simplify complexity shows itself in sometimes unexpected frugality. "When we first got into business," he recalls, "I had more money than brains, so I had really nice offices. Then I saw we didn't need them, and we moved out." Today his office contains two tables; one is used for meetings; the other serves as his desk. Both are cafeteria models that cost a total of $300. A few ratty old chairs complete the décor. When a staff member tried to replace the chairs, Parsons insisted they be returned.

I asked if his Spartanism was a signal to his team or simply an expression of his personal taste. A bit of both, Parsons told me. It's a reminder of where the company came from, he says, adding that fancy furniture doesn't make money. "It's the people, your systems, your ideology, and your culture that matters."

The mandate to engage with customers by keeping things basic and simple governs Go Daddy's vision and shapes its operations. In the Internet business, Parsons told me, the possibilities are limitless. "You can fly off in a billion directions, so it's really important to stay focused." Wheel spinning has stalled dozens of major Internet companies that expanded into one new area after another, only to discover they weren't doing well in any of them. After spending millions of dollars to get their ill-fated ventures up and running and then trying to sell them to customers, they looked up to see competitors advancing seemingly out of nowhere to overwhelm their core product or service. Parsons avoids that kind of fatal mistake by decreeing that every project or proposal must involve or improve the use of the domain name. If not, Go Daddy stops it dead in its tracks.

Appraising Go Daddy's future, Parsons has his eye on the whole world. About 20 percent of its business is already international, and he anticipates more. Hunting trips in Africa and India have persuaded him that English is a universal language and that GoDaddy.com's audience is international. He predicts that someday every newborn child will receive a domain name good for a lifetime. He can't wait for the future and all its changes. And why not? He sees Go Daddy as "the on ramp to the Internet."

When I asked Parsons if he thought he could hold off his competitors, he answered with the studied logic of a Marine who served with great distinction in the Vietnam War: "Our generals looked at those rice paddies, and they saw the water was a foot deep. What they didn't realize was that, underneath the water, the mud was 3 feet deep. Not so easy navigating. The same goes for Go Daddy's Internet businesses. They seem easy to get into, but they are really deep and muddy. Lots of companies big and small have tried, and they've made zero impact."

In other words, to its customers, Go Daddy seems to be a straightforward, uncomplicated business. But behind the scenes, incredible complexity exists. However, with his ability to think creatively and his fierce management style, Parsons makes it all look simple.

RULES OF ENGAGEMENT

▶ *Train your eye on customers' unmet needs and quirks.*
Parsons ignored tradition by starting a business before he had figured out his market, product, and business model. He tested the Internet waters by simply plunging in to see if he could swim. That's a risky approach—one that I would not normally advise. But Parsons was packing a life

preserver—his keen judgment. He knew instinctively that helping customers solve the complexities of the Internet was an enormous opportunity to be grasped. He could see their unmet needs.

Parsons was right, and, for whatever reason, most of Go Daddy's competitors seemed to lack the same basic understanding of the human condition. New—and even mature—technologies are often difficult for customers to navigate. What technologists and laypeople see as "simple" is not always the same. This divergence creates a rich field of business opportunity for simplifying technology's complexity.

If you choose to take Parsons' approach to building a business, you will be developing your company's competencies at the same time you are out in the market assessing the unmet needs and idiosyncratic behaviors of your potential customers. You will be looking for a match between competencies and needs.

NEW—AND EVEN MATURE—TECHNOLOGIES ARE OFTEN DIFFICULT FOR CUSTOMERS TO NAVIGATE. WHAT TECHNOLOGISTS AND LAYPEOPLE SEE AS "SIMPLE" IS NOT ALWAYS THE SAME. THIS DIVERGENCE CREATES A RICH FIELD OF BUSINESS OPPORTUNITY FOR SIMPLIFYING TECHNOLOGY'S COMPLEXITY.

► *High-tech requires high touch.* A naïve view believes that technology-based businesses can be programmed to run on their own. Just create a sophisticated Web site that anticipates all possible customer questions and problems, and let the customer do the work. For a complex service or product, I have never seen this strategy work.

Parsons quickly recognized that customers who have problems need access to real people. "When it comes to communicating and doing research and conducting business, people love to use the Internet," he told me. "But when it comes to learning to do something and solving problems, people much prefer to deal with people."

▶ *Go beyond the ordinary with service.* If your engagement proposition is based on good service, good just isn't good enough. Your standard of performance needs to be substantially better than that of your competitors to sustain your market position and to get the attention of potential customers.

IF YOUR ENGAGEMENT PROPOSITION IS BASED ON GOOD SERVICE, GOOD JUST ISN'T GOOD ENOUGH. YOUR STANDARD OF PERFORMANCE NEEDS TO BE SUBSTANTIALLY BETTER THAN THAT OF YOUR COMPETITORS TO SUSTAIN YOUR MARKET POSITION AND TO GET THE ATTENTION OF POTENTIAL CUSTOMERS.

Parsons makes it very easy for people to get what they need from his unusually well-staffed Customer Care centers. But he takes his service proposition a giant step further with his Office of the President concept, designating a group of highly trained team members to handle the most complex, high-level questions. And as Assistants to the President, they carry the weight of importance that exceedingly demanding questioners require.

It is a brilliant strategy for engaging with customers. Real problems get real attention, fast. Customers hang up the phone with an abiding sense that they matter to the company. Relationships are cemented, word-of-mouth spreads, and new business flows.

▶ *Metrics matter.* Parsons didn't invent the idea, but it bears endless repetition. You can't really gauge the efficiency of your company's marketing program, and other operations, unless you closely track the metrics. If you do that, you will also enjoy a significant side benefit called the observer effect, which refers to the changes that occur in certain behaviors when someone is keeping tabs on them. In business, the observer effect occurs when people in the company see what you're tracking. What you measure signals what's important and the outcome you're aiming for. People get it, and soon they are coming up with ideas designed to advance your goals—assuming that you have the right people on the job.

Another side benefit of good metrics is their ability to reveal where performance breakdowns reoccur. If you track breakdowns, you can start to identify the systemic problems in your program that you must fix.

WHAT YOU MEASURE SIGNALS WHAT'S IMPORTANT AND THE OUTCOME YOU'RE AIMING FOR.

THE FIRST INKLING OF A BUSINESS OPPORTUNITY CAME TO HONEST TEA'S FOUNDERS, BARRY NALEBUFF AND SETH GOLDMAN, IN 1994, WHEN NALEBUFF WAS TEACHING AND GOLDMAN WAS STUDYING AT THE YALE SCHOOL OF MANAGEMENT. NALEBUFF, A PROFESSOR OF BUSINESS STRATEGY, WAS DISCUSSING A STUDY OF BOTTLED DRINKS WITH GOLDMAN, ONE OF HIS TOP STUDENTS, WHEN THEY CONVERGED ON A FACT THAT CAUGHT THEIR ATTENTION: ALL NONDIET DRINKS EXCEPT BOTTLED WATER—NOT JUST SODAS, BUT FRUIT JUICES, SPORTS DRINKS, AND ICED TEAS, TOO—WERE LOADED WITH SUGAR, USUALLY IN THE FORM OF HIGH-FRUCTOSE CORN SYRUP. EVERY MAJOR NATURALLY SWEETENED DRINK ON THE MARKET HAD THE EQUIVALENT OF 10–12 TEASPOONS OF SUGAR IN A SMALL CAN OR BOTTLE.

CHAPTER 6
WHAT COULD BE MORE INSPIRING THAN HONESTY?

In marketing terms, sugar sells. Food packagers usually find that the more sugar they can add to almost any food product, the bigger their sales. Whether it's good for customers is another matter. Well-known nutritionist and best-selling author Marion Nestle calls bottled drinks "liquid candy," and the harm they do extends not just to decaying teeth, but also to the obesity and diabetes epidemics that now plague the United States.

Acutely aware of the health issues, Nalebuff and Goldman were personally frustrated by their inability to find bottled drinks that weren't overly sweet. At the same time, they were struck by the obvious market opening created by the uniform overload of sugar. Given a choice, most people don't use more than a teaspoon or two of sugar in their tea or coffee. And it's a good bet that few consumers, health-conscious or not, would freely choose as many sugar calories as the drinks provide. Clearly, the right product could exploit that disparity with a drink sweetened only lightly. Both men liked the idea, but Goldman, a runner who had long despaired of finding a really refreshing drink to imbibe at the end of a jog, was particularly excited by it.

After their discussion at Yale, Goldman and Nalebuff half-joked more than once about the company they would found to make a low-sugar, bottled drink. They even explored mixing natural fruit juice with carbonated water and a touch of sugar, but any drink made with real juice would be too pricey to compete in a market in which the contents of most products cost hardly anything.

The critical piece dropped into place in 1996 when Nalebuff flew to India to write a case study of the Tata Tea Company and

discovered the intricacies of that country's vast tea market.
He found that what most American consumers know as tea
is actually the sweepings and fannings left over after the
good leaves are packaged for more discriminating palates.
Particularly when used in bottled iced tea, the leavings make
for a bitter, unpleasant taste. However, U.S. bottlers such as
Snapple actually seek out the most astringent teas, because
anything less pungent loses all flavor when mixed with 10
teaspoons of sugar.

As with fine wine, Nalebuff told me, really good tea might cost
a hundred times as much as the cheap stuff. Still, even the
best tea costs only pennies a pound, and a pound of tea will
make 62.5 gallons of Honest Tea. "Good tea is one of the world's
cheapest luxuries," he explains.

The business case was undeniable: A bottled drink made with
quality tea would cost just a bit more than one made from the
sweepings, and it wouldn't need as much sugar to mask the bad
taste. In addition, a bottler using one-tenth as much sweetener
could afford to buy a better form of it—honey or maple syrup,
perhaps. And a tea that promised fewer calories and a healthier
drink could command a premium price from health-conscious
consumers. It would be a new kind of venture, violating every
fixed tenet of the bottled-drink game. So be it. Nalebuff realized
that this was the product that he and Goldman had long
envisioned.

By coincidence, Goldman called Nalebuff shortly after the
professor returned from India, and he once again raised the
subject of a subtly sweet drink. "He asked if I remembered

2007
52 EMPLOYEES

We launch 9 new products, including Honest Kids organic thirst quenchers: Berry Berry Good Lemonade, Goodness Grapeness, Tropical Tango Punch; Pomegranate Red Tea with Goji Berry; Sublime Mate; Pomegranate White Tea with Açaí and Honest Ade Orange Mango with Mangosteen.

Honest Tea makes the cover of *Beverage Industry* Magazine.

Honest Tea partners with Jamis Bikes to give away 500 bikes to consumers, and one to every Honest Tea employee.

Honest Tea moves to new environmentally-friendly headquarters, making our local contribution to sustainability.

sales $23 million

You can see the complete history of Honest Tea by going to **www.honesttea.com**—including the most recent announcement that the Coca-Cola Company has bought 40% of the company. It's an Incredible acknowledgment of the market power and purity of Honest Tea's brand.

2007 – We welcome new investors and board members with the launch of nine new products. New flavors that have already hit the shelves include Pomegranate White Tea with Açaí and the newest Honest Ade, Orange Mango with Mangosteen, both in plastic, and Sublime Mate (Honest Tea's first yerba mate drink) and Pomegranate Red Tea with Goji Berry in glass. Our Just Green and Just Black are the first of our teas available in 64-oz. bottles. This spring we will be launching our much-anticipated new line, Honest Kids, with three flavors of low-sugar organic thirst quenchers—Goodness Grapeness, Tropical Tango Punch, and Berry Berry Good Lemonade!

2008 – We celebrated our 10th anniversary in February and also announced that The Coca-Cola Company purchased 40 percent of Honest Tea, presenting opportunities for even further growth and expansion nationwide. Five new flavors included Citrus Green Energy Tea, Peach White Tea, Lemon Black Tea in 16.9 oz. PET bottles, as well as Citrus Spice Decaf and Jasmine Green Energy Tea in 16 oz. glass bottles. Consumer Reports again ranks Lori's Lemon as the best bottled tea in its May issue...

the idea about a low-calorie beverage," Nalebuff recalled, and wondered if "I'd ever done anything with it. I told him I hadn't, but that now I was ready." In short order, Goldman assumed the title of CEO (or Tea-EO, as he likes to say). "Seth has been the person who's really completely responsible for taking the idea and making it happen," Nalebuff graciously claims. Well, not completely: Nalebuff came up with the brand's clever name.

Certainly, a company called Honest Tea would need to live up to its name if it wanted to truly engage its customers. That prerequisite dictated the strategy for the company's wholly unorthodox business model. Honest Tea would be real tea, made by real people, starting with Goldman and Nalebuff themselves, and their signatures would appear on every bottle. The bottle itself would display a tasteful, understated main label, a jujitsu-like engagement tactic to make Honest Tea stand out from its garish competitors on grocery shelves. The back label would contain a chatty, slightly nerdy message explaining the drink and its history to the buyer. And, most important, truth would be the touchstone for everything that was said and done in making and marketing Honest Tea. Total transparency in all aspects of the operation would be the means of engaging with customers.

After raising $500,000 in start-up money from family and friends, the partners began experimenting with some fairly exotic brews of tea for family, friends, colleagues, and students to sample. They soon realized they were too far ahead of American tastes when one of the tasters in a focus group hired to sample the winners implored, "I know you're paying me to drink this, but do I have to?" With that, Nalebuff and Goldman regrouped, falling back on flavors that are more recognizable and acceptable to American palates—flavors such as mint, blood orange, and lemongrass. They also gave their drinks catchy names such as Tangerine Green, Just Black, and Peach Oo-la-long.

The partners' breakthrough came when Fresh Fields, a health-food chain that Whole Foods Markets has now acquired, sampled five flavors and ordered 15,000 bottles. After a search, Goldman and Nalebuff located a manufacturing plant that could brew and bottle their teas the way they wanted. And early in 1998, Honest Tea was in business.

However, attracting customers was a major problem in the early days. Similar to Stonyfield's Gary Hirshberg, Goldman and Nalebuff had no money for promotion. And they suspected that advertising would be counterproductive anyway because their target customers, having been fooled by products pretending to be healthy, were deeply skeptical of any such claims. As with Hirshberg's approach at Stonyfield, their solution was to distribute truckloads of point-of-sale samples.

"Once [consumers] tasted it and understood what we were doing, they knew right away," Nalebuff says. The typical reaction was, "Where have you been all my life? This is exactly what I've been looking for." Then the freshly minted Honest Tea drinker would go off to spread the word among friends. The transparency tactic worked so well to engage customers that Goldman and Nalebuff had to budget time to answer e-mail messages from their fans.

A TEST FOR THE TRUTH TELLERS

With truth as its credo, Honest Tea encountered its first big test when a new drink called Zero (a name meant to dramatize the calories it didn't contain) was ready to go on sale. The labels were literally at the printer's shop when the partners discovered that their fermented cane sugar sweetener would add 3.5 calories to each bottle. Under U.S. government regulations, anything below 5 calories can be rounded down to 0 in labeling and advertising. No one would need to know that Zero didn't quite live up (or down) to its name. But for Honest Tea, the discrepancy was crucial. "We couldn't call it Zero if it was 3.5," Nalebuff says. "So we changed the name and the product, too." Making the drink just a bit sweeter and adding some agave juice to jazz up the flavor and boost the calorie count, the partners called it Ten.

In hindsight, that was the point at which the relationship with the customer began to outweigh the product—or, as Goldman puts it, when "[we] became more about the honest and less about the tea." Their customers wanted a product that would make them feel good about their own bodies, their ethics, and their stand against an often dishonest world. Filling that need became the company's top priority.

Still, Goldman and Nalebuff didn't lose their perspective. As at every company profiled in this book, hardheaded practicality is a constant at Honest Tea. However strong its dedication and whatever the purists might say, the company never lets desire to engage with customers overrule the facts of the marketplace. Two key incidents illustrate the point:

1. Early on, Honest Tea found a delicious red tea called honeybush that was grown in Haarlem, South Africa, by a community of independent farmers using a grant from the United States Agency for International Development (USAID). "This was exciting," Goldman explains. The story seemed custom-tailored to engage Honest Tea's customers. "It was a real model of community-based economic self-sufficiency," he says.

2. Honest Tea introduced its Haarlem Honeybush drink and promised a share of the revenues to the growers. But the drink didn't sell well. "It was too much about the mission and not enough about what our customers wanted to drink," Goldman told me. So the label was scrubbed. Angry customers sent e-mails: "How could you do this? You're just like all these other corporations!" But since then, the company has introduced its Pomegranate Red Tea with Goji Berry that uses the same honeybush leaf, and the growers in Haarlem have received more income from that drink than they ever got from the first one. "What's the better choice for that community?" Goldman asked—to stick with the failing label or move on?

3. In 2003, Honest Tea marketed its first Fair Trade drink, a product that guarantees its Third World growers a share of the proceeds larger than that of non-Fair Trade products even when market prices drop. The arrangement seemed to be a good way to strengthen its engagement with customers, and the company set out to calculate what it would cost to make all its drinks Fair Trade. It turned out that a wholesale changeover would raise costs by 50 percent, forcing either a disastrous product-price increase

or a profit margin so small that Honest Tea's business would be unsustainable.

4. Some staffers insisted that the company do the "right thing" by sharing proceeds at the designated rate no matter what. But Goldman argued that the growers wouldn't be helped if sales collapsed or Honest Tea went out of business. Since then, the company has added six Fair Trade labels converting more items to Fair Trade certification each year, which do indeed help the growers without endangering the company. It has delivered on in its Fair Trade promise by carefully—and fairly— negotiating with growers on their share of the profits.

If Honest Tea had been a nonprofit venture supported by donors, it might have struggled on with Haarlem Honeybush and made a ruinous wholesale switch to Fair Trade suppliers. But with investors to answer to, Nalebuff and Goldman had to gauge the marketplace. And in the end, all parties were better off.

Similarly, the partners decided early on that they wanted their entire line to be organic. Apart from its ideological appeal, the move was a natural extension of their original push for healthy products. "Most people don't realize that tea leaves are never rinsed," Goldman told me. "The first time any chemicals on the leaves are washed off is when hot water is poured on them to make tea, so the chemicals end up in the tea. With organic tea, there are no chemicals to drink."

Price wasn't a problem—even though top-quality organically grown tea costs as much as $5,000 a ton, considerably more than even the best conventional tea. The switch worked because a ton of tea stretches so far that the organic tea in a 16-ounce bottle costs only about 4¢. What blocked the conversion initially was a shortage of the product itself. The market didn't have enough organic tea to meet Honest Tea's bubbling demand. But a significant number of Indian and Chinese growers had switched to organic methods after a scare about pesticides in tea swept through Europe during the mid-1990s, and, eventually, enough organic tea was coming to market to enable Honest Tea to put the label on all its drinks.

Ten years after its launch in 1998, Honest Tea comes in 18 flavors, and it's available across the country on store shelves at Whole Foods, some Target stores, regional supermarket chains, and a wide assortment of co-op markets, eateries, and convenience stores. The company, which has grown by more than 70 percent a year for two years running, sold more than 30 million bottles of tea in 2007. Revenues totaled $13.5 million that year, putting Honest Tea comfortably in the black for the first time. Sales in 2007 totaled more than $23 million, up 72 percent. Word of mouth, much of it generated by the transparent way the company does business, drives its sales; Honest Tea advertises in only a few trade journals.

Representatives of a certifying agency accredited by the U.S. Department of Agriculture inspect production at every step— from the tea gardens to the company's bottling plants. Each tea grower's paperwork must be verified and pest-control methods approved, and the plantations must send a copy of their certification with every shipment of tea. At the bottling plants, organic products cannot be manufactured at the same time as nonorganic goods. Before every organic batch is processed, the equipment must be flushed out and sanitized.

Clearly, Honest Tea's engagement with its customers inspires the company. Keeping its promise of total transparency matters more than what the company sells. Decisions are made not on the basis of scientific marketing strategies, but on how the decisions fit with the brand and what it stands for. To the company's customers, "Honest" is now synonymous with organic and healthy products sold by an enterprise that is true to its word in every way. The power of that combination in the marketplace trumps any market research—and it puts Honest Tea in marked contrast to traditional marketers that polish their brands, not their companies, to a high patina. At Honest Tea, truthfulness about all things is the one-and-only way to engage with customers.

Being totally transparent has also enabled Honest Tea to turn every facet of its operation into an opportunity to fulfill that mission. If you're committed to an organic lifestyle, Honest products fit the bill. If you care about fair compensation for workers on faraway tea plantations, you've come to the right place. If healthy eating is your cause, ditto.

Venture capitalists clamored for years to invest in the privately held company, but Goldman and Nalebuff politely declined. They had seen other companies expand too fast, with no clear plan or an organization solid enough to support growth. Not until early 2007 did Honest Tea accept a new $12 million round of financing to launch a major expansion—one that underscores the point that Honest Tea is more about the first word than the second. The company already produces a line of Honest Ades—lightly sweetened fruit drinks in flavors that range from cranberry to lime that outsell Honest Teas in parts of New York City. Now the company is introducing another product: Honest Kids juice pouches meant to compete in school lunchboxes with the ultra-sweet Capri Sun line.

The Honest Tea payroll has nearly tripled to a still-lean 48 people, and the company has moved into big new offices outside Washington, DC. Tellingly, however, the new digs look and feel like the old ones, with an open layout and no private offices. And the partners still make decisions to fit the brand promise, not scientific marketing. For example, Honest Kids juice pouches have a full day's supply of vitamin C and only 40 percent of the calories of the rival Capri Sun pouches. If the competing lines had been tested on kids in focus groups, Goldman told me, there would have been no contest: "They would have said, 'I like Capri Sun better.' Well, no kidding; it's loaded with sugar. It's like the Pepsi challenge; of course a kid will like it better." But at every trade show and tasting, he explained, the Honest Kids product has "blown people away. Like, oh my gosh, they get it right away. They understand why it makes sense. It hits people over the head. So I've never been more confident about how our product will do in the market."

Given today's heightened environmental and healthy-lifestyle awareness, Goldman sees nearly limitless opportunity for new products that mesh with Honest Tea's goal of engaging customers through its transparency. They could introduce new products "across the board, wherever it makes sense, wherever the mainstream alternatives don't meet that criterion," he adds. "It doesn't have to be just beverages." Only half in jest, he recalls a customer's voice-mail saying, "I wish you did everything; I wish you did my banking; I wish you were my neighbors."

Any new line of Honest products must be organic, healthy, and faithful to the Honest Tea promise. That last criterion, being the most subjective of the three, is hardest to define and enforce, but, luckily, Goldman and Nalebuff have a truth detector in Goldman's wife, Julie. She recently read the earnestly green copy on a competitor's bottle of tea and said bluntly, "That's such a load of crap. These guys talk about saving the world, and they're really talking all about themselves." She was right, Goldman told me, and her truth detector is always attuned to marketing claims, both those made by rivals and those made by Honest Tea. "We'll work on some label language and I'll show it to her, and she'll say, 'No way.'" The text gets revised until Julie approves.

Goldman and Nalebuff are committed to keeping the transparent connection with their customers. By putting their signatures on every Honest Tea bottle, they personify the product. That's why they stay up nights answering the many e-mails from customers reading, "Dear Seth and Barry." To "Jim" who complained that his neighborhood stores didn't carry Peach Oo-la-long, colloquially known as Opus, Goldman recently replied: "Dear Jim, Opus is very much alive and well as Peach Oo-la-long. I am not sure why you are having trouble finding it. Please let me know where you are geographically, and we will try and fix the problem. Thanks and regards, Seth."

And, like most of the men and women I interviewed for this book, the partners agree that they are having fun. They are engaging their customers, and two reassuring events in recent months prove it. First, Jones Soda, a $500 million company and a real threat, introduced a line of bottled tea that got no traction; second, Honest Tea now outsells Tazo, the Starbucks brand that used to be the market leader. Like Honest Tea itself, life in a fast-growing company might not be totally sweet, but it's refreshing—not to mention fulfilling and exhilarating.

RULES OF ENGAGEMENT

▶ *Make sure your message is authentic and represents who you really are.* When you are engaging with customers by being honest, the converse also applies: Everything you do must be true to your message.

WHEN YOU ARE ENGAGING WITH CUSTOMERS BY BEING HONEST, THE CONVERSE ALSO APPLIES: EVERYTHING YOU DO MUST BE TRUE TO YOUR MESSAGE.

▶ *Tailor your message to your market.* In the beginning, healthy refreshment was Honest Tea's promise, and the obvious customers were people who were already interested in healthy eating. The partners sold through a health-food chain and relied mainly on guerrilla marketing, persuading store managers to pass out samples of their drinks and relying on customers to tell their friends about them. The formula worked.

However, as time passed, the partners realized that the connection they were making with customers was "more about the honest and less about the tea." Their promise was really transparency and truthfulness for customers disillusioned by conventional marketing. A customer sipping an Honest Tea was not just taking healthy refreshment, but was standing up against hype and dishonesty.

I am struck by how many companies misrepresent the truth about what they deliver to customers. A recent advertisement by British Airways (BA) illustrates the point. "Be a guest, not just a passenger," it proclaims, going on to say: "We believe that the way you fly is just as important as where you fly. It's not just about getting a seat, it's about getting service."

At the time this ad was running, BA passengers were suffering through what might have been the worst customer service in air travel history as they tried to fly through London's Heathrow Airport. After BA and the London Airport Authority opened a new terminal, a BA flight took off for Paris not with just a few bags missing, but with absolutely no luggage in the cargo hold. Customers bitterly complained about the lack of information concerning the snafu. BA's ads should be apologizing to customers and telling them how it will fix its all-too-apparent problems instead of fantasizing about a quality of service that doesn't exist. That would be honesty.

Honesty widens the scope of your markets. A platform of genuine honesty enables you to broaden your offerings to customers. Having established that platform, Goldman and Nalebuff were able to branch out from tea to a wider market in fruit drinks and juice pouches—and, eventually, perhaps, to still other products and services.

▶ *Take your cue from your customers.* A platform built on honesty requires a close engagement with customers; you must stay in tune with their feelings, beliefs, and needs. Wisely, the Honest Tea partners listened to their customers and dialed back from the unusually flavored teas they originally wanted to market. And when their mission led them to overtax their customers' tastes with the Haarlem Honeybush line, they withdrew it—but without abandoning their African growers.

▶ *Keep your promises.* Your engagement with customers is a promise that you must keep if you hope to maintain their loyalty. In Honest Tea's case, nothing less than total honesty and transparency can fulfill the commitment. Therefore, government-approved inspectors regularly scrutinize its whole operation. And even though government regulations would have allowed Honest Tea to market its so-called Zero product that actually contained 3.5 calories, Goldman and Nalebuff knew they had no choice but to stop its development and rethink the product.

▶ *Be pragmatic.* In the real world, too much idealism can be a handicap; you must balance it with reality. Honest Tea couldn't go totally organic until growers were producing enough organic tea, and it couldn't go totally Fair Trade without a ruinous rise in costs. By waiting and compromising, Goldman and Nalebuff found a way to serve their customers, their suppliers, and their bottom line as well.

IN THE REAL WORLD, TOO MUCH IDEALISM CAN BE A HANDICAP; YOU MUST BALANCE IT WITH REALITY.

ACCORDING TO THE FIRST PRINCIPLE
OF MARKETING, LAUNCHING A NEW
PRODUCT BEGINS WITH IDENTIFYING THE
TARGET CUSTOMER'S NEEDS. YOU THEN
SHAPE THE PRODUCT TO FIT THOSE
NEEDS. BUT BECAUSE YOU'RE OUTSIDE
THE CUSTOMER'S HEAD LOOKING IN,
YOUR PERCEPTION OF YOUR TARGET'S
MIND IS SUBJECTIVE AND MIGHT BE
COLORED BY YOUR OWN HOPE FOR A
SALE. TIME AFTER TIME, A NEW PRODUCT
FAILS BECAUSE YOU DON'T KNOW YOUR
CUSTOMERS' REAL NEEDS UNTIL THEY
EXPERIENCE THE ACTUAL PRODUCT,
AT WHICH POINT YOU MIGHT DISCOVER
THAT THERE ISN'T A FIT.

CHAPTER 7
WHAT COULD BE MORE INSPIRING THAN BEING YOUR OWN CUSTOMER?

One solution—although it's not available to everyone—is to become a customer yourself so that you're looking out instead of in. When a marketer identifies with customers' lives and expectations, perceptions often coincide and new products succeed.

One of the best examples I know of this kind of engagement— certainly the most touching—is the story of Two Little Hands Productions, a mixed-media company that turns the sign language of the deaf into a language that all children and their families can delight in. Two entrepreneurial sisters, both mothers, created the company by sharing their own experiences with other mothers, some who have hearing-impaired children and others who simply believe that signing benefits all children. For Two Little Hands Productions, the engagement with its customers is so natural and so profound that it erases any division between marketers and customers: It's just mothers helping mothers, building a nationwide business in the process.

The story begins with Rachel Coleman, then a musician and member of a folk rock band, and her husband, Aaron. In 1996, the Colemans fell deeply in love with their smiling new baby, Leah; they simply couldn't get enough of her. Often they took her to noisy concerts and let her sleep while Rachel performed. They never needed a babysitter because she slept peacefully through screeching, stomping, thumping, and twanging loud enough to wake the next county.

Product Overview

Signing Time Series One and Two (26 DVDs Total)
Recommended Ages: 1-8+
Play, sing, and sign along with Signing Time while learning American Sign Language (ASL). This multi-sensory DVD series introduces children to a "hands on" second language.
Featuring Rachel Coleman and her daughter Leah, who is deaf, along with Alex (Leah's cousin, who can hear) and their animated pet frog Hopkins, the Signing Time series teaches hundreds of ASL vocabulary-building signs that are useful in daily life. Content includes teaching segments, original songs, charming animation, plus real families demonstrating each sign in the proper context.

Baby Signing Time Series (4 DVDs Total)
Recommended Ages: 3-36 months
Babies crawl before they walk, and sign before they talk! With Baby Signing Time, babies can express their needs and wants using simple signs long before they can speak.
Featuring Emmy-nominated host Rachel Coleman along with Leah, Alex and Hopkins (animated as babies), Baby Signing Time uses clever songs to teach over 100 of the most useful signs for daily wants and needs.

Practice Time Series (2 DVDs)
Practice Time ABCs and 123s include unique DVD features that enable children to participate in interactive quizzes as they practice the manual alphabet, fingerspelling , numbers and counting with Signing Time star, Rachel Coleman. The Practice Time DVDs can be used as companions to the Signing Time series or on their own.

Signing Time Music CDs
All of the original music from the Signing Time and Baby Signing Time series is available on music CDs. Songs are available on CDs or in a downloadable mp3 format .

Signing Time Board Books and Flashcards
Our easy-to-use books and flashcards help reinforce reading skills while practicing basic ASL signs. Use alone or as a companion to Signing Time DVDs.

The work of Two Little Hands Productions responds to the deep and compelling needs of its customers. When you go to its Web site, **www.signingtime.com**, you will be engaged as if you were a member of the family.

The baby's ability to sleep through any kind of racket seemed odd, but she was more than a year old before the Colemans finally got it: Leah was profoundly deaf; she couldn't hear anything, not even her mother's singing.

The Colemans were not remotely defeated, but their lives instantly took a very different turn. "My priorities changed," Rachel told me. As the daughter of a composer father who had worked with clients ranging from Sonny and Cher to The Jackson Five, music had been a part of Rachel's life since childhood. But now there would be no room for it; if Leah couldn't hear, Rachel would give up singing, performing, and songwriting. "I put down my guitar and picked up sign language," she says.

Well-meaning friends warned that children who sign might never learn to talk, but Rachel and Aaron were intent on communicating with their child as quickly as possible and in whatever form worked. Their daughter had already lost a year's worth of normal development, so they had no time to lose.

The Colemans began with a system that translates English words directly into signs. It worked for them, but it obviously meant nothing to Leah. "She didn't understand it," Rachel said. "She didn't know English." That became clear when Rachel signed, "Leah, look at the red car." The sign for "look" includes pointing in the required direction, so as soon as Leah saw it, she looked toward the red car. But when Rachel signed "Leah, red car, look," the message got through. So Rachel switched to American Sign Language (ASL), which uses a sophisticated interior logic and grammar to fit the world of the deaf. With tutoring help from a deaf adult friend, both Rachel and Aaron soon mastered ASL.

At 15 months, an age when typical toddlers are pointing and whimpering to signal their wants, Leah could sign, "Mom, I want a grilled cheese sandwich and chocolate milk. Thanks. I love you." When Leah was two, she and her parents were chattering away so easily with their hands that her vocabulary soared and she began reading written words—long before others her age were even close to reading.

Rachel's sister, Emilie Brown, was so touched by Leah's progress that she and her husband, Derek, began teaching sign language to their own infant son, Alex, so that he could eventually converse with his cousin. Emilie began with simple words—*milk, more, mom, dad, sleep.* Alex started signing back when he was nine months old. It was wonderful, Emilie remembers: More than a year before she expected him to communicate clearly, he was emerging as a true person in his own world. "You discover who your child is and what matters to him. You find out that his favorite thing to drink is actually orange juice, not milk." Studies show that signing can boost a child's IQ and speed development, she says, "but the real impact comes in everyday life. You have a child that can communicate, and you are sure he has learned something." For a parent, that's pure joy.

With challenges enough to overwhelm many parents, the Colemans were about to be handed still more. Leah was three years old when her mother became pregnant again. An ultrasound test showed that the baby had spina bifida, a cleft in the spine that typically causes paralysis. Rachel had intrauterine surgery, and 10 weeks later baby Lucy was born. She appeared to be a normally child with only a slight numbness in her legs. Nine months later she was diagnosed with cerebral palsy. It was a devastating blow, but Rachel characteristically refused to give up hope. She kept talking, singing, and reading to the unresponsive child. "She was locked in her body," Rachel said, "but I knew Lucy was in there."

The next leap forward came when Leah was four years old. The sisters and their families were now living next door to one another in Los Angeles, and three-year-old Alex often went to preschool for the deaf with Leah. But apart from close relatives, Rachel told me, "very few people in our lives were learning sign language. Most people around us felt intimidated by Leah, even the adults." She wasn't invited to birthday parties because parents were afraid they wouldn't know when she was hungry or had to use the bathroom. Children were reluctant to play with Leah because she couldn't hear them and they didn't understand her signs. One boy requested that the soccer coach not pair him with Leah at practice, explaining that "she can't hear me, and she can't even talk." Although Leah was sweetly oblivious, Rachel was standing right there, absorbing those hurtful words about her daughter.

Pragmatic as always, Rachel said she "wasn't mad at anyone," but four-year-old Leah was getting left out of life. The situation would only worsen as she got older. "What can I do to change this?" Rachel asked herself. She started volunteering at a preschool for hearing kids in her neighborhood, conducting weekly story times that included simple signs in ASL. Within weeks, children who previously had merely stared at Leah's signing were including her in their games. "Two signs, 'play' and 'friend,' completely changed their world," Rachel remembers. "When I saw that, I got excited."

But there was a catch: What would happen when Rachel wasn't right beside Leah to intervene? "I can't do this all her life," Rachel admitted to herself, "just follow her around and teach all the kids she gets involved with."

At this point, Emilie and her family had moved to Virginia, so the sisters had to be content with long, daily phone calls to stay in touch. One day Emilie had an idea: Why not use their shared musical background and savvy to make a video for kids? They would use music to educate children. Better yet, it would give the sisters a reason to get together.

That's when Rachel had her eureka moment: "Great idea, but first we need to do sign language."

"You get chills," Emilie told me, "then you say , 'Yeah!'" Emilie knew of young mothers in many communities who had begun signing with their perfectly normal babies or toddlers before the kids could speak actual words. The trend was sparked by studies that show children can use their hands and fingers to communicate long before they can speak; it's natural and fun just liken when parents and children play hand games.

Emilie immediately latched onto Rachel's video idea as a potentially powerful way to, as she put it, "make a difference in Leah's world." The video could teach signing to parents of hearing children, while vastly expanding the range of communication for deaf children such as Leah.

It took a year to produce *Signing Time—My First Signs*. Originally, the sisters planned to have the two children teach the signs as the word being taught was spoken aloud and spelled out on the screen to reinforce the message. The demonstration would be followed by animated pictures of the word in question and images of other children repeatedly signing it. But at the first editing session, it was clear that Alex and Leah, then just three and four, were too young to clearly demonstrate the signs from a teaching position for the 30-minute show. So Rachel, with her performer's voice and larger-than-life smile, stepped in as the central figure who introduced each new sign and anchored the video.

A former colleague of Emilie's who ran a production company was enlisted to produce the video. The first video was just about wrapped up when Emilie prodded Rachel into reconsidering her decision to leave music behind. "I know you say you're not a singer or a performer or a songwriter any more," she said, "but you're the closest thing we've got. So go write us a theme song." Bowing to the inevitable, Rachel borrowed a guitar and took Lucy and the guitar into a nearby room. Just 25 minutes later, she emerged with two tunes—the first a theme song with the same title as the video, and the second an almost prayerful expression called *Show Me a Sign*. "Show me you're in there," was the message, "prove your doctors wrong; tell me you're okay." "Tell me that you love me. Tell me that you're thinking of me. Tell me all about the things you are thinking day and night. Tell me that you're happy, and you love it when we're laughing. Tell me more," it pleaded. "Oh tell me more. Show me a sign. Show me a sign." The theme song drew instant applause, and *Show Me a Sign* had everyone in tears. The sisters decided to play *Show Me a Sign* during the credits at the video's end. Their keen instinct for authenticity, a powerful tool for engaging with customers, was on display.

In April 2002, a month before the first video was released, Rachel was playing it at home with Lucy in her arms. When the video ended, Lucy knocked one fist against the other. Rachel watched in awe as her daughter signed "more." "She willed her hands to open, and she started signing," Rachel recalled. "Then she started talking." A mother's wish had been granted, but Rachel also recognized that Lucy's accomplishment pointed to a whole new market for signing videos: Children with delayed development, Down's syndrome, and other special needs could clearly benefit from signing instruction. (Today eight-year-old Lucy, although in a wheelchair, is fluent in both ASL and English and is a fully engaged and happy member of the Coleman family.)

At the beginning of this adventure, Rachel told me, she would have been content just to make 100 copies of the video and give them to people who knew Leah, thus changing her daughter's immediate world. But Emilie, who always had an entrepreneurial streak, had other ideas, including a well-thought-out concept of *Signing Time*'s premise: "You and your child will watch this video together. We don't have to promise that your child will be smarter. You'll see it, just as we have with our own children." So the sisters incorporated as Two Little Hands Productions and set up a Web site, Signingtime.com, which was followed by an association with Amazon.com to sell the Two Little Hands videos.

Before long, Amazon customers were raving about the video, and Aaron Coleman had given up his job as a parks supervisor to help with the company and later joined the production team to film and edit more offerings. But without start-up capital, the first year of filming was quite a scramble. "We got by on credit cards and favors from friends and family," Emilie says.

The big break came in February 2003, when NBC's *Today* show did a segment on Rachel and *Signing Time*. Fortunately, the sisters had known for about six months that the segment was in the works, and the company had geared up for a surge in production and shipping. Still, they were surprised and gratified by the volume of orders that poured in after the show aired. *Signing Time* became the top-selling video on Amazon.com that day pushing *My Big Fat Greek Wedding* and *Harry Potter* from the top spots. Rachel was interviewed in *Ladies Home Journal,* which unleashed a steady stream of stories and media interviews about the company, its founders and their families, and the videos that introduced them to a broader audience.

Two Little Hands had become a real business, one whose 2006 sales reached $3.1 million, which translated into nearly 500 percent growth in just three years. Rachel and Emilie turned what many misunderstood as a crutch for the handicapped into a tool that helps all children to share a language that opens life and learning to everyone. And at every step of the way, they have done it by remaining true to their own experience, convictions, and instincts. They profit from who they are and the authenticity that cements their engagement with customers. The marketing strategy, Rachel told me, is simply this: What do I wish there was to fill a need for Leah or to change the world to suit her better? "It's not just for Leah; it's for so many other families," Rachel says, "but it meets our needs as well."

Looking back at their media debut in 2003, when NBC's admiring *Today* show turned the sisters' story into a public relations dream, Emilie put her finger on the Two Little Hands' appeal: It is the singular aspect of its engagement with customers and the consequent trust it engenders. In effect, the customers perceived the owners as customers themselves. "We were our own demographic," Emilie says. "What made a huge difference was the organic nature of the product coming from Rachel's life. It wasn't the usual case of, 'Hey, let's make something the market wants.' Our real success came from making something that matters to us—really, really matters— and that we can share with thousands of other parents in the same boat."

What's ahead for Two Little Hands Productions? The sisters aren't sure. "How long it makes sense for Alex and Leah to do this, how many original episodes need to be produced to satisfy the market, those are questions we don't know for a fact," says Emilie.

Whatever the sisters decide to do, they are determined that it will be something that comes from their own authentic experience. "We just made what we needed and it worked, because we know what we need, and we are no different from every mom out there," Emilie reflects. Of course, in developing TV shows, they consult a panel of experts and advisors. "We have to play that game now because of what's at stake," Emilie told me. "But just because some researcher says you should do it this way—if it's not entertaining, if it doesn't feel right, if it doesn't have heart, if it doesn't work for our kids, we are going to try something else." In the end, she says, "I don't need a researcher to tell me that it works. I know it works."

RULES OF ENGAGEMENT

▶ *Remember that empathy pays.* The great advantage of being a customer of your own product or service is that you automatically have empathy for other customers. You understand what they are going through. You understand their needs. You are extremely sensitized to how various offerings can fulfill those needs (or not). It's an important principle for all product and service developers, regardless of your engagement strategy.

I've actually seen companies treat their customers with hostility. They see their customers as too demanding, wanting too much, and willing to pay too little. It is an unfortunate and unprofitable condition in many business-to-business relationships. A classic example is the relationship, or lack thereof, between automobile manufacturers and their component suppliers. The contentious relationship between these parties keeps both from being as profitable as they could. They have little empathy for each other's situation—just a push to get the most that each can wring out of the other, even if one of the parties fails.

Could a hard-headed executive from Detroit learn anything about empathy from Two Little Hands? Try this: Never regard customers as aliens from another class or culture, never unfairly take advantage of your customers or suppliers, identify and respect everyone's values and expectations, and treat everyone as friends and pilgrims in an increasingly complex world.

NEVER REGARD CUSTOMERS AS ALIENS FROM ANOTHER CLASS OR CULTURE, NEVER UNFAIRLY TAKE ADVANTAGE OF YOUR CUSTOMERS OR SUPPLIERS, IDENTIFY AND RESPECT EVERYONE'S VALUES AND EXPECTATIONS, AND TREAT EVERYONE AS FRIENDS AND PILGRIMS IN AN INCREASINGLY COMPLEX WORLD.

▶ *Keep a little distance if you do get inside your customer's head.* Being too close to a customer need might cause you to lose perspective. Rachel and Emilie have been successful because they intimately understand the needs of hearing-impaired children and their playmates. But they also stood back from their venture to get a sense of what would work in their markets; they were not driven only by their needs. They were also able to put themselves in the shoes of others.

▶ *Trust your intuition when you are inside your customer's head.* That's the way Rachel and Emilie operate. Plenty of experts are always ready to provide you with advice. Just remember that they've formed their opinions based on what they know; you might know more or know something readily applicable to the business you are trying to build, and the experts' knowledge might not fit your situation. It's especially true if, like Rachel and Emilie, you are venturing into new territory.

But never stop weighing the advice of experts against your own experience and intuition. If you disagree with what they are telling you, don't stay silent; argue with the advice giver. The truth might lie somewhere in between what you and others think. For your business to remain successful, you must stay as close as possible to the truth about your customers.

BUT NEVER STOP WEIGHING THE ADVICE OF EXPERTS AGAINST YOUR OWN EXPERIENCE AND INTUITION. IF YOU DISAGREE WITH WHAT THEY ARE TELLING YOU, DON'T STAY SILENT; ARGUE WITH THE ADVICE GIVER. THE TRUTH MIGHT LIE SOMEWHERE IN BETWEEN WHAT YOU AND OTHERS THINK.

▶ *You can commercialize an idea even if it emerges from a high sense of purpose.* Commercialization might seem to violate the grand purpose that spawned a great idea. But unless you get a product or service into the marketplace and sustain its supporting business, the idea won't benefit anyone but you. There is nothing wrong with making a profit, even when you started your company to bring about some greater good. In fact, you need profits to invest in the growth of your business, and you are always free to decide what to do with any excess profits. A moral or social purpose can coexist with commercialization.

IT'S CALLED THE BIG GREEN EGG®,
AND THAT'S PRECISELY WHAT
IT LOOKS LIKE: AN OVERSIZED
EGG—GREEN WITH A DIMPLED
SURFACE, STANDING ON ITS
CHOPPED-OFF SMALL END, AND
PROPPED UP ON SPINDLY METAL
LEGS. IT'S AN IMPROBABLE
OBJECT OF DEVOTION. YET
HUNDREDS OF THOUSANDS OF
EGGHEADS ARE EAGER TO TELL
YOU THAT IT'S THE BEST DARN
BARBECUE GRILL AND SMOKER
THIS SIDE OF ANYWHERE.

CHAPTER 8
**WHAT COULD BE MORE
INSPIRING THAN ENTHUSIASTIC
CUSTOMERS?**

If you've never heard of the EGG®, it only means that none of your friends, relatives, or neighbors own one. Eggheads are tireless promoters who tell anyone and everyone that the ceramic cooker, derived from an ancient Oriental design, is the best possible way to prepare anything from steaks, fish, and hamburgers to slow-roasted brisket, smoked meats, cornbread, or even a cherry pie. In fact, the Egg also stands as a monument to Ed Fisher's persistence as well as his mastery of two arts: not just designing a cooker, but also persuading his customers to engage everyone they know to buy Eggs of their own. This kind of engagement is painstaking work and often slow; but for the right product, it's magic.

Starting in 1974, Fisher's dogged persistence led him to build a customer list for his Big Green Egg Company (BGE) one satisfied person at a time. At first, he demonstrated his evolving product to folks who stopped in at his retail store in Atlanta; later he began giving samples to potential distributors he met at trade shows and industry meetings. Almost everyone who sampled the cooking succumbed to Fisher's charms—or, rather, to the charms of his endearingly oddball cooker. The result was a constantly expanding flock of Eggheads who, after they tried it, couldn't seem to stop crowing about the succulence of the food it produced, attracting additional acolytes to the congregation of Egg worshippers.

Along the way, Fisher tinkered with his cooker until he had a product that was ready for national distribution—but even then, he didn't trust mass marketers with his hatchling. Only carefully selected specialty retailers capable of educating customers in using and caring for Fisher's peculiar contraption were allowed to handle his precious Egg.

EGGtoberfest

Click here to view a short video detailing the EGGtoberfest EGGsperience!

EGGtoberfest is an annual event held the third weekend in October in Atlanta. It originated in 1998 as a way for Big Green Egg to say "Thank You" to loyal customers that regularly logged on to the Forum to chat and share recipes and experiences and found themselves becoming fast friends. Many were eager to meet their online "family" and EGGtoberfest provided the opportunity to get together, cook their favorite recipes on the EGG® for everyone to sample, and swap stories about life experiences - good and bad. The first year about 100 Big Green Egg pioneers attended the cookout, which was held at the American Legion Hall in Atlanta, with 15 cooks firing up an EGG. The meet, greet, and eat event turned into the First Annual EGGtoberfest, which was considered a big success.

You might have missed the 2008 EGGtoberfest, but it's not too late to get to the next EGGtoberfest. Just go to **www.biggreenegg.com** to see a video about the EGGsperience.

Who—other than Fisher himself—could have guessed that an odd-looking product with an equally offbeat marketing strategy would turn into a growth company extraordinaire? But the privately held BGE has done just that. Its double-digit sales growth has doubled so many times over the years that BGE now owns the kamado cooking market, describing itself on Biggreenegg.com as "the world's largest producer and international distributor" of the ceramic cookers. Fisher says that sales in 2008 are expected to again surpass record 2007 sales to attain yet another milestone.

A MIRACLE WITH FLAWS

The Big Green Egg story begins in Japan, where a visiting Fisher first sampled food prepared in the kamado style of cooking. A tried-and-true technique perfected over 4,000 years, kamado traditionally uses clay pots or earthen pits to produce juicy, flavorful meals. Fisher was so taken with the Japanese fare and its ease of cooking, compared to the familiar American tradition of barbecuing on metal grills, that he decided to start his own clay-cooker business when he got back home. A lot of Japanese-made products were coming into the United States in the 1970s, Fisher told me, and he started his cooker business by importing and selling the Japanese kamado pots.

"I demonstrated the product in the front of my store," Fisher recalls, "cooking up batches of food and giving away free samples." It was a great way for a guy with no marketing budget to introduce people to an unfamiliar cooking concept while also building his own credibility with potential customers. Not only did the charcoal-fired kamado turn out tasty food, but it also was fast—fast to start up, fast to cook, and fast and easy to clean. People loved the miracle pot and raved about it to their friends, who, in turn, would come in to Fisher's store and pick up a kamado of their own. "Each cooker became a salesman for me," he said.

Even so, the kamado wasn't an instant success. One-to-one selling was a laborious way to market a product, and the pots were somewhat fragile, often had defects, and required a lot of maintenance. Fisher was reluctant to expand. The imported cookers weren't initially something Fisher could build a business on, he admitted to me—at least not an expanding business that would include stores in other cities. Fisher keenly values his reputation for good customer service, and he knew that a flawed or fragile product such as the one he was selling was bound to stir up complaints and problems that he'd have a hard time solving. If he wanted to grow, his cooker had to evolve.

Thus began a ten-year saga that included a search for the right manufacturer and a drawn-out learning process to design the perfect cooker, which morphed from clay into a more durable, heat-resistant ceramic material, the same one used in the NASA program. Loyal customers gladly pitched in to help Fisher come up with the best design. (To this day, BGE involves customers in product design and improvement and also solicits feedback from dealers.) The customers shared their cooking experiences and suggested changes. What finally rolled off the assembly line was the Egg—not yet exclusively green, but an "original American-designed ceramic cooker," as the company describes it.

The improved cooker still uses charcoal (Fisher recommends natural hardwood lump charcoal, not briquettes). Just ten minutes after lighting, the Egg can fire up to 750° to sear a steak. But thanks to a sophisticated system of vents and dampers, it can also cook at temperatures as low as 200°. And its thick ceramic walls retain heat so well that it can cook or smoke foods for 24 hours straight without needing additional charcoal. An easily read exterior thermometer shows the inside temperature, and the controls can keep the heat steady within a few degrees of the target level.

Eggs now come in five sizes—from the Mini, with its 9-inch diameter grill, to a monstrous XL that weighs 205 pounds and can hold two 20-pound turkeys. They're pricey, up to $900, with a full line of optional "Eggcessories" ranging from specialty grills, tongs, and spatulas to fire starters, rib racks, seasonings, mitts, DVDs, and a baking stone for pizza. (A suggestion to offset the higher price, which we always like to tell consumers: Since the ceramics have a lifetime warranty, owners should never need to replace this grill, making the price an actual bargain.)

Eggs come in well-cushioned packing crates that can safely be shipped to customers and retailers around the country. When Fisher got the Egg out to a broader market, the customer-engagement phenomenon picked up speed. Egg owners just can't stop cackling about their cookers, and they are articulate advocates for the product.

Fisher's search for the right manufacturer eventually led him to Dal-Tile Corporation, a subsidiary of Mohawk Industries, which manufactures, distributes and markets high-quality ceramic tile and natural stone products. Dal-Tile is the largest ceramic tile manufacturer in the U.S. and one of the largest tile manufacturers in the world. The job Fisher was proposing was only superficially similar, but his chosen supplier was willing to learn how to make what he wanted. In addition, Fisher liked the fact that Dal-Tile had the sophisticated laboratory facilities needed to design the various ceramic components of the Egg. They had to fit together perfectly to perform to Fisher's specifications —not an easy task with ceramics because they dry at different speeds, depending on the configuration, and might shrink or twist after leaving the kiln. Then they needed to create the paint: A special type of epoxy paint made from glass had to be concocted to give the Egg the appearance and durability Fisher demanded.

Dal-Tile solved those and many other problems to Fisher's satisfaction, which is why he has stayed with the same supplier for more than 20 years, even though its ownership has changed hands. The people Fisher knows and trusts are still there. He told me, "It's through their expertise that we can continue to innovate, improve, and maintain the quality of the Egg." Fisher prides himself on being loyal to his customers, dealers, and suppliers, and his reward is their dedication and engagement with the company and each other.

The Egg paint that Fisher's supplier mixed originally came in a paint box of colors. But one day, while Fisher was talking to a local salesperson about putting together a newspaper ad, he pointed to one of his Eggs by way of description. It happened to be green, Fisher's favorite color, and the notion of calling the cooker and the company "the Big Green Egg" was hatched. Call it serendipity, but what better name for a product than something catchy and completely descriptive? "People remember it," Fisher says with perfect simplicity. No Marketing 101 professor could put it better.

In the early years, sales of the Egg slowly spread to neighboring Florida and other surrounding areas as people took their cookers with them when they relocated or vacationed in nearby states. As word spread, dealers began to get inquiries from customers hunting for Eggs and contacted Fisher to place orders. Before long, more dealers became intrigued as Fisher himself, the truest of the true believers, showed off his Eggs at home and at trade shows, always cooking up a feast of appetizers, main dishes, and desserts to show people the full range of this strange contraption.

Gradually, the Big Green Egg went from being the smallest of niche players to a real powerhouse in the upscale grill industry. Fisher engaged his customers so thoroughly that they became the core of his sales crew. But as he was quick to remind me, the customer buzz wouldn't have lasted for long if he hadn't kept his part of the bargain. The credibility that he painstakingly built with his customers played a big part in his growing and lasting success. "Not only was the product good," he pointed out, something that performed exactly as Fisher told people it would, "but we were able to ship on time and to do whatever else was necessary to have a satisfied customer on the other end."

These days, the rapidly growing BGE gets outside help from
DHM Group, Inc., a company that acts as a sort of outsourced
marketing department. But BGE still doesn't rely on traditional
advertising campaigns because, as Fisher tells me, the Egg
is not a product that people can easily relate to without
some previous interest or knowledge and some hands-on
training and demonstration. Instead, the marketing efforts
leverage BGE's enormously effective customer-engagement
strategy by carefully choosing vehicles that already attract the
knowledgeable cook—magazines such as *Bon Appétit* or *Fine
Cooking,* for example. And in a free-publicity scenario that
the average product promoter can only dream about, savvy
magazine editors looking for the new-new thing in the sizzling
world of gourmet cooking often come to the Big Green Egg
for information and photos that they can incorporate into
magazine features.

Dealers in the specialty barbecue, pool and patio shops where
the Egg is sold appreciate the enthusiasm and loyalty that keep
customers coming back. And the dealers themselves are an
extraordinary bunch—more like BGE partners, really—who
need to be willing to give the Egg special handling because
its shape and carefully fitted components make it prone to
breakage if service people get careless. The dealers need to give
potential customers special handling, too. The uninitiated must
be shown how this odd-looking implement works and how to
cook with it for the most satisfactory results. Egg dealers need to
know enough about it to answer any questions. Obviously, the
required special handling is not something that the typical big-
box store or Internet dealer would or could manage to Fisher's

satisfaction. That's why BGE allows only specialty retailers to distribute its product.

Fisher is well aware that his distributors and dealers need to lavish more attention on his Eggs, and BGE recognizes and rewards them for their loyalty by offering much better margins than most of the other high-end grill companies. The dealers also like the fact that they don't need to compete with big-box retailers, for whom low pricing is the clarion call.

Donna Meyers, the founder and CEO of the DHM Group marketing company, likes to say that Egg owners would turn over "their truck, and their dog and their other prized possessions before they'd ever consider giving you their Egg."

She might be right. The Egghead community is a tight-knit group, and BGE nurtures and guards the Egg mystique on its Web site, the biggreenegg.com Forum, where Eggheads spend untold hours communicating with one another. Each day, 400–900 Egg lovers post messages on the Forum. They share cooking tips and recipes, answer questions, and extol the virtues of their Eggs. Their testimonials are so effective that dealers often send potential customers to the site to read the unedited comments of adoring fans or to tap BGE's extensive cache of Egg lore. Fisher thinks the extensive consumer education aspect of the site, along with the burgeoning Web site activity, has played a big part in the company's accelerated growth in recent years.

BGE rewards and encourages this family-like behavior by using some of the customer testimonials in its marketing brochures, catalogs, and trade ads. The Web site's display of Egg buyers' devotion is also a powerful tool for attracting new distributors.

But the event that may best illustrate how lovingly the company nurtures its bond with its Eggheads is its 11-year-old annual Eggtoberfest. Held on the third weekend in October at the company's new world headquarters in Tucker, Georgia, the event originated in 1998 as a way for BGE to thank those loyal customers who regularly log on to the Web site to chat and share their Egg-cooked dishes. In 2008, more than 1,700 people enjoyed the annual reunion with their online Egghead family members. From 15 cooks firing up Big Green Eggs in 1998, the event has grown to more than 230 Eggs cooking everything from fresh-caught Alaska salmon to Maine moose kabobs.

So much fun and enthusiasm is generated at the Eggtoberfests that regional Eggfests are springing up around the country (currently 19 regionals).(While the number will keep changing, I think that great a number indicates that almost anyone can find an Eggfest near them.) Apparently, you can't keep a good Egg down, as Fisher knew nearly 35 years ago when he started his partnership with his adoring customers.

RULES OF ENGAGEMENT

- ▶ *Credibility counts.* Anyone can profess a strong belief in his or her product, but Fisher understood that building his company's credibility with both customers and distributors was paramount to his success. Particularly when you rely primarily on engaging your customers to do your marketing, you cannot risk having a dissatisfied buyer tear down your slowly and painstakingly built reputation. And these days, when information moves at Internet speed, an unhappy customer or two can do a truckload of damage to a product's reputation. That is the dangerous side of the Internet phenomenon.

To keep the Egg's image shiny bright, Fisher engages a team of talented product developers and designers—reinforced with feedback from Egg users and distributors—to constantly improve the product and add new Eggcessories. He also makes sure that the company maintains on-time shipping and provides customer service that is second to none. And because BGE's credibility is so tightly woven with his distributors' performance, Fisher recognizes and rewards his dealers for the extra attention they give Egg customers and the knowledge they must acquire to educate potential buyers. Remaining credible requires excellence in everything you do—and you need constant vigilance.

▶ *Be realistic; keep your eyes wide open.* When both you and your customers share an uncompromising zeal for your product, it's possible that your rose-colored glasses will prevent you from seeing product defects or problems. Defects or problems that remain unaddressed can turn customers into cynics. Furthermore, I have always believed that zealots can quickly convert to equally powerful critics when things go wrong, so balance your enthusiasm with reality and be sure that issues get addressed.

ZEALOTS CAN QUICKLY CONVERT TO EQUALLY POWERFUL CRITICS WHEN THINGS GO WRONG, SO BALANCE YOUR ENTHUSIASM WITH REALITY AND BE SURE THAT ISSUES GET ADDRESSED.

Fisher is his product's biggest booster. But he also understands that the Egg has its drawbacks: Its unusual shape affects its stability and its composition requires special handling. Instead of ignoring the problems or trying to gloss over them with less-than-honest advertising, he does what he can to alleviate the drawbacks and then accepts the remaining faults as part of the bargain. One way that he offsets the Egg's shortcomings is by insisting that only specialty retailers handle the product.

Fisher never considered a big advertising campaign because he knew that his oddball product couldn't be explained in the typical television spot or mainstream magazine ad. Egg customers need more information, the kind that only hands-on demonstration and training can provide. Fisher understands that proper education is the key to creating satisfied Egg buyers, and mass-market retailers could never provide all that is required. Knowing that any instant riches attached to mass marketing would be short-lived, at best, he foregoes them in favor of keeping a smaller number of customers happy. Not all great ideas are meant for the mass market.

▶ *Nurture your mystique.* Egg owners have an air of exclusivity and mystique. Customer engagement grows with the feeling of belonging to a special community centered on a product that not everyone knows about. BGE reinforces this sense of community with its Web site, its Forum for bringing Eggheads together, and its special events. The Eggcessories not only bring in added revenues, but also give Eggheads more tokens of their shared identity. Part of any product's mystique often lies in exclusivity. So as your product presence grows, you will need to find similar techniques to maintain engagement.

▶ *Faith and perseverance pay off.* What's so inspiring about this tale of customer engagement and the phenomenal power an enthusiastic crowd can bestow on a product is the unusual faith Fisher displayed as he moved from being a small niche player to a powerhouse in the grill industry. That kind of faith is essential; if you are not completely sold on your product, customers and distributors won't be, either. Fisher was so completely convinced of his Egg's superiority that he never gave up. In these days of overnight cyber-success stories, it's refreshing to see that hard work and perseverance can still pay big dividends for those whose faith never wavers. It's what a crusade inspires.

▶ *Choose your channel partners carefully.* Earlier in this book when I described the engagement strategy of MemberHealth, I said that if your channels to market touch your customers, make sure that you know the people and companies in these channels—and that you trust them. A product or service that requires special attention in the distribution or selling process requires channel partners that are equally committed to your standard of quality. A Big Green Egg is not just a product—it's an experience. And everyone who touches the product or customer contributes to that experience. The principle is clear: Choose your partners carefully.

A PRODUCT OR SERVICE THAT REQUIRES SPECIAL ATTENTION IN THE DISTRIBUTION OR SELLING PROCESS REQUIRES CHANNEL PARTNERS THAT ARE EQUALLY COMMITTED TO YOUR STANDARD OF QUALITY.

WHEN JOCHEN ZEITZ TOOK THE HELM
OF THE GERMAN SPORTS SHOEMAKER
PUMA IN 1993, HIS FIRST PRIORITY WAS
SURVIVAL. THE COMPANY HAD GONE
THROUGH FOUR CHIEF EXECUTIVES IN
AS MANY YEARS. AFTER EIGHT STRAIGHT
YEARS OF LOSSES, IT WAS MIRED IN DEBT
AND WAS BEING HOPELESSLY LAPPED
BY INDUSTRY LEADERS ADIDAS, NIKE,
AND REEBOK. WORSE, NO ONE EXPECTED
ZEITZ TO SUCCEED. AT 30, HE WAS AN
APPRENTICE BY EUROPEAN STANDARDS,
THE YOUNGEST CEO OF A PUBLICLY
HELD GERMAN COMPANY. *MANAGER*
MAGAZINE PREDICTED HE WOULD
"CRUMBLE UNDER THE PRESSURE."

CHAPTER 9
**WHAT COULD BE MORE
INSPIRING THAN THE MELDING
OF COOL AND SPORT?**

Reminiscing, Zeitz said recently, "When you look at the photos, you think, I was so young. How could anyone give me so much responsibility?" But as Puma's marketing manager, he had made a solid pitch to the board, and the directors saw no better choice. Luckily, control of the company was then in Swedish hands; German owners never would have taken a chance on him, he says. "At the time I didn't feel scared or anything," he recalls. "I was just very excited." And Zeitz did what was needed: He launched a classic restructuring that peeled away layers of bureaucracy, laid off 400 employees, closed the German factory, and moved production to Asia. Within three months, Puma was showing a profit.

But all that, Zeitz knew, was merely emergency surgery. Puma had survived, but if it were to succeed, much less compete with adidas and Nike, it needed a long-term strategy. Above all, it had to inspire its customers to forge a tight and lasting connection with the company. Zeitz found his strategy—and the way it has worked to make Puma the world's third-largest sports apparel company is a classic story of inspiration and authenticity.

IF THE SHOE DOESN'T FIT

Puma's long conflict with adidas amounted to fratricide. The companies were founded by brothers, Adolf and Rudolf Dassler, who had inherited their father's shoe business in the tiny Bavarian town of Herzogenaurach in the 1930s. They scored an early victory when Adolf, known as Adi, took a suitcase full of track shoes to the 1936 Berlin Olympics and persuaded

America's star, Jesse Owens, to wear them during his triumphal refutation of Adolf Hitler's racist creed. But the brothers fell out. By one account, Rudolf became convinced that his brother had contrived to have him sent to the front during World War II, and Rudolf retaliated by telling the victorious Allies that Adi had collaborated with the Nazis.

Despite their feud, the brothers cohabited in a villa with their families until 1948, when Rudolf and the workers loyal to him split off to form the company that became known as Puma. Adi renamed the original company adidas, and Herzogenaurach became a town of warring factions, with loyalists on each side who wore only the "right" brand of shoes, kept to their own stores and taverns, and sometimes refused to speak to people on the other side.

Over the years, the two companies competed viciously. They sponsored dozens of professional teams, especially in soccer, and waged bidding wars for star endorsements. In a move that still echoes in Olympic competition, they shrugged off the rules and went after potential medalists with cash and favors. In her 2008 book *Sneaker Wars,* author Barbara Smit reports that during the 1968 Olympics in Mexico City, adidas agents somehow managed to get Puma shoes impounded by Mexican customs and may even have arranged for a Puma representative to be arrested and jailed.

The intensity of the war between adidas and Puma seems to have blinded both to the rise of Nike and Reebok in the 1970s, and the German companies lost ground. adidas's U.S. market share dropped from 60 percent to just 2.5 percent in 1990, and

There's plenty of action on the Puma website, **www.puma.com**. You can see new products, be inspired by athletic feats and prowess, and imagine yourself flying through the air—on wings of Puma sneakers, of course.

Puma fared even worse. The heirs of Adolf and Rudolf got along
no better than the brothers had, and both companies passed
out of family control.

These days, Zeitz and current adidas CEO Herbert Hainer take
the competition a good deal less personally. But the rivalry
is still there, and it irritates. adidas bought Reebok in 2005,
giving it a 26 percent share of the global market against Nike's
33 percent. By contrast, Zeitz's solo strategy has clawed Puma
back from near-oblivion to a 6 percent market share, with sales
of $3.2 billion—and he's determined to gain enough ground to
make it a genuine three-way race again.

Back in the early 1990s, when he settled on his strategy, Zeitz
knew that head-on competition in the classic sports shoe
market would be a losing game. Puma was simply outgunned
by the big players, which could sponsor more and better teams
and buy endorsements from bigger stars. So he bet big on
an untried gambit to inspire a wider universe of customers,
stretching beyond sports: Puma would focus not on the
performance of its shoes, but on fashion for people who cared
about performance. "We had to position the brand as edgy and
design driven," he says. "By doing this, we changed the formula
of the industry. We created the term *sports lifestyle*." Despite
the fact that no one knew what that meant, Zeitz set up a new
sports lifestyle division. And he hired an uninhibited 21-year-
old skateboarder, Antonio Bertone, to run it and experiment
with fashion innovations.

PUMA WOULD FOCUS NOT ON THE PERFORMANCE OF ITS SHOES, BUT ON FASHION FOR PEOPLE WHO CARED ABOUT PERFORMANCE.

Luck lent a helping hand in 1994, when members of the Beastie Boys appeared in concert wearing blue-suede Puma Clyde sneakers. That line hadn't been hot since the 1970s, when it was named for New York Knicks basketball star Walter "Clyde" Frazier, but the rap band's nostalgia trip inspired its fans to comb stores for Clyde sneakers. In the midst of his move to Asia, Zeitz ramped up production. And when major U.S. retailers turned up their noses at what they saw as a passing fad, Bertone cruised clubs and concerts, handing out Clydes to trendsetters and pitching them to urban boutiques, where sales took off.

Frazier was far from the only star in Puma's galaxy. In its heyday, before the financial woes, the company had bought endorsements from soccer stars Pelé and Diego Maradona, and football's Joe Namath, among others. Zeitz's next big break came in 1998, when rising designer Jil Sander called and asked if she could use Pelé's classic soccer boot in a fashion show. Zeitz was delighted. Sander's minimalist style was the antithesis of conventionally flashy sports design, and he saw her interest as a chance to revamp Puma's image, inspiring a whole new group of customers with no previous interest in sports shoes. She made Puma attractive again—and in short order, Puma was marketing a Jil Sander line, working variations on its classic sneakers with new textures and edgy colors. And when Madonna appeared on a magazine cover wearing customized

Pumas with three-inch heels, Zeitz ordered up another line of shoes featuring the singer's style. He sponsored skateboarding's World Cup and ventured out of sports altogether to back the Berlin Love Parade, a rave festival.

Meanwhile, Bertone was pushing beyond shoes to sports apparel. Puma turned out a catsuit for tennis star Serena Williams and a one-piece uniform for the Cameroon soccer team. The international federation banned the outfit, but Zeitz defends it as a worthy technological innovation: "It was the lightest jersey that has ever been created." Puma has become the prime producer of driving shoes and auto-racing suits, and it recently launched a line of sailing clothes. Zeitz has also begun collaborating with a string of diverse designers, ranging from Alexander McQueen and Philippe Stark to Mihara Yasuhiro and Hussein Chalayan, and with model Christy Turlington and jeans maker Evisu. Their designs in upscale outlets have engaged and inspired a new class of customers, raising Puma's gross profit margin above 52 percent.

To be honest, all this seems more a cacophony of styles than a cool, rebellious image, but Zeitz sees the mélange as an actual advantage, forcing his in-house designers to keep reimagining their work from many points of view. The celebrity designers "come at it from completely different angles," he says, "and I think that's what helps Puma constantly keep an open mind." Creativity that fuses fashion and performance, Zeitz maintains, is a far better innovative tool than market research. With research, "all you will get fed back is a perception of today, not tomorrow," he says.

Puma's sort of creativity can be as fruitful as it is risky. In 2002, Bertone bought 600 pounds of vintage clothing and had it refashioned into a limited-edition line called Thrift, a seemingly nutty idea that evolved into an online, customized-sneaker business called Mongolian Shoe BBQ. "I always describe working for Puma as, 'They give you all the rope in the world to hang yourself with,'" Bertone deadpanned. "Your job? Don't hang yourself." More recently, the company has ventured beyond shoes and apparel. Puma now has a line of aluminum-cased luggage for business travelers and, in partnership with London designer Vexed Generation and Danish bike maker Biomega, Puma offers a hot-selling, foldable urban bike that has been exhibited at New York's Museum of Modern Art.

For all the company's diversity and fearless experimentation, Zeitz is highly conscious of its roots in the sports shoe business, and he has been careful to preserve the brand's authenticity with real sports fans. As his treasury has expanded, he has moved back into direct competition with adidas and Nike by sponsoring 32 national soccer teams (12 of them in the latest World Cup competition, 5 in the European championship) and supporting star athletes whose endorsements sell shoes. In a marketing triumph at the 2008 Beijing Olympic Games, Jamaican sprinter Usain Bolt won three gold medals wearing Pumas—and then took off the golden shoes and kissed them while photographers snapped away. "It wasn't something we staged," Zeitz said later. "He did it because he really identifies with Puma."

In fact, Zeitz insists that Puma's association with Bolt is "something that you can't translate into money. We picked him up very early when he was nobody—just a great talent—and really believed in his potential and stayed with him. We made him a hero in our global advertising campaign without knowing he would have a breakthrough at the Olympics." Still, the payoff is real: "Those visuals and images go around the world, and there are very few that haven't seen them."

In 2007, Puma's comeback story inspired and engaged a different kind of customer: Francçois-Henri Pinault, the French luxury-goods tycoon whose PPR empire includes the Gucci, Yves St. Laurent, and Stella McCartney brands. Pinault became a customer for the company itself, paying €3 billion ($4.2 billion) for a 62 percent stake in Puma. But Puma continues to operate as an autonomous company, and Zeitz says the relationship is "nothing but positive."

Lean and rangy at 44, Zeitz could personify the Puma brand: He still runs marathons, flies his own plane, has an estate in Africa, and speaks seven languages, including Swahili. And he's very much in charge of his company. "The changes haven't affected me. The strategy is the same," he says. In the narrowest of terms, that means "to grow our business again and to close the gap with the two leading brands." But in a broader sense, Puma's strategy is to lead, not follow, the competition. "We always try to do extraordinary things and push the boundaries," Zeitz says. "We constantly need to change ourselves to stay ahead of the game."

PUMA'S STRATEGY IS TO LEAD, NOT FOLLOW, THE COMPETITION.

For all the changes, however, the brand must stay true to itself—a new kind of authenticity that goes far beyond testimonials to athletic performance. For athletes and ordinary customers alike, Puma is about looking good in a distinctive, sporting way—or, as Zeitz puts it, "It's about fashion and styling, and not just blood, sweat, and tears." That means he can't just sign up the next hot designer or any potentially record-breaking athlete. "We pick designers and athletes because they fit the Puma profile," Zeitz explains. "Their personality needs to work with the brand. We don't say, 'He's fast.' We say, 'He has a lot of potential and fits the Puma brand.'"

Usain Bolt's celebratory antics in Beijing, where he broke the world records for both the 100-and 200-meter sprint, raised some eyebrows and drew a sour reproof from Olympic Committee Chairman Jacque Rogge. But Bolt inspired millions around the world when he kissed his shoes, draped the Jamaican flag around his shoulders, and did a hip-swiveling dance around the "Bird's Nest" national stadium. That was the authentic Puma—and it was the real payoff on Zeitz's investment.

RULES OF ENGAGEMENT

- ▶ *Build on your past.* Puma has leveraged its sporting past by building on the power of its brand and the mystique embodied in its history. As with legendary gun maker Smith & Wesson, another diminished legacy company that I wrote about in *Outsmart!,* the first book in this series, a dying Puma has been reinvigorated by a new CEO,

Jochen Zeitz, who knew which part of the company's past was worth keeping and what had to change. And in an appropriately feline coincidence, Zeitz was following a principle set down by the Sicilian author of *The Leopard*, Giuseppe di Lampedusa, who wrote, "If we want things to stay as they are, things will have to change." Under Zeitz's brilliant guidance, Puma has inspired customers old and new by holding on to the best parts of its past and changing the rest.

Throughout its makeover, Puma has stayed true to its legacy as a maker of shoes for serious sport, while developing a style that appeals to a broad cross-section of consumers. At almost every track-and-field event and World Cup soccer match, the Puma brand is very visible, both on the playing fields and in the stands.

"IF WE WANT THINGS TO STAY AS THEY ARE, THINGS WILL HAVE TO CHANGE.—GIUSEPPE DI LAMPEDUSA"

▶ *Don't try to go head-to-head with entrenched market leaders.* Business is too tough to challenge competitors at their own game. Take on competitors laterally by finding another distinctive way of getting into the market. Puma did it by developing a unique image of edgy cool.

You can also look for a distinctive frame of reference for your company. Puma never directly entered the sneakers war; it defined itself as a sports lifestyle company and then built an apparel and shoe business that could challenge adidas and Nike. Alternatively, you can simply look for something that you can do better than your competitors. Puma, for example, had no trouble besting the tired image and styles of Reebok.

▶ *Use outsiders to challenge insiders.* If you want to keep refreshing your product line at a rapid clip, you may need more design capacity than you can keep in-house. Besides, an inside design group can get bogged down in old industry paradigms and often needs to be challenged. Puma broke through the lethargy by engaging celebrities to generate new ideas. Sometimes new ideas work and sometimes they don't. Customers are key to the experiment, the ultimate judges of what's cool and what's not. It's another way of keeping them coming back, as long as cool prevails most of the time.

▶ *Follow a well-marked highway, but also test side roads now and then.* Puma keeps its edgy style but tests many designs consistent with that style. Its designers come from different worlds of "cool"—sports, art, architecture, and fashion, to name a few—which ensures that the customer experience is anything but boring. When customers enter a Puma outlet, they experience a smorgasbord of consistently edgy cool that engages ages 6 to 65, and they keep coming back because they know things are going to change. It's a reflection of Lampedusa's revelation that things have to change if we want the overriding experience to stay as it is.

Iconic brands achieve this balance of consistency and change. Despite all the change it has undergone, Puma's style remains very recognizable. This summer, I bought a pair of sneakers at the Puma outlet store in Kittery, Maine. They are about as daring as I get when it comes to fashion: dark green with orange laces and an orange Puma logo. When I wore them on a trip to France, people kept asking where I got my cool Pumas. I will go back to the Puma store because the styles make me feel younger.

▶ *If you're the underdog, play it up.* Remember, people like the underdog. They will come to your aid and buy your products if they are good. It's gratifying to engage in the campaign of an underdog. Puma played its underdog role well, adopting a feisty, scrappy image. Then it tamed the image for some product styles to broaden their appeal. The last time I went into a Puma store, most of the apparel and sneakers still had a feisty edge, but there was also an elegant white jacket with the BMW Racing Team logo. The more conservative turn suggested that the underdog had gained considerable ground.

▶ *Keep your edge authentic.* For all the companies featured in this book, authenticity is necessary to keep customers coming back. At Puma, authenticity is about always presenting an edgy coolness while staying rooted in serious sport, a two-pronged requirement that most apparel companies don't have to meet. When an athlete wears a Puma jersey or sneaker, the pullover or sport shoe must work well while also looking good. It should enhance the performance of the athlete while also inspiring an amateur to think she can perform like a pro.

For me and for entrepreneurs everywhere, it's inspiring to see a legacy company like Puma that can balance everything needed to rebuild itself and still maintain its edge in terms of fashion and athletic competition.

This book described the great opportunities that lie before us and what's possible for businesses that grasp those opportunities. But I am a realist as well as an optimist. As this manuscript goes to the publisher, a dark cloud hangs over us. People the world over fear that an extended recession has set in.

The headlines of today's newspaper say it all: "Big and Small, Companies Cling by a Thread." The stories describe how a local plastics company is being hit by higher materials costs while orders are falling; how a large national retail chain is closely managing its liquidity; and how a third corporation, unable to extend its financing, must do more belt-tightening in order to survive. There is even a story of how a local university has frozen hiring and stopped all construction on campus, concerned that the increasing financial needs of students will force the school to draw on its assets.

The current crisis has been created by tight credit—for banks, for businesses, and for consumers. But concerns about a recession were building even before global credit markets began to stagger. A worldwide slowdown had already begun and signs of overcapacity were showing up in many industries. As Charles Darwin would have put it, businesses have been breeding beyond the pool of available customers. I have always wondered why anyone needed three Home Depots within a

EPILOGUE

10-mile stretch of highway near my home. Now, Home Depot is asking the same question.

A global economic slowdown certainly gets leaders focused. The most immediate response is to reduce costs: shutter plants, lay off people, drive down supplier prices. But as one CEO put it during the last recession, you can't shrink yourself to greatness. Even in challenging times, it's important to think about innovation and growth.

The auto industry has been battered mercilessly over the past year or two, but history teaches that the industry is often inspired to new creative heights by adversity. When air-quality regulators in the United States and Japan and sky-high gasoline prices were making life miserable for automakers in the 1970s, Honda bet the bank on the low-mileage Civic and won big. Facing bankruptcy in 1979, Chrysler introduced the minivan. Sales rose dramatically, and Chrysler came back. Even now, there are signs that 2010 will be a breakthrough model year with a rash of new hybrids and all-electric vehicles. For those outfits that have built up a cache of cash, a downturn is prime time for expansion. Increased market share may come from acquiring hard-hit competitors.

Of course, not every company will be able to seize the opportunity to innovate or expand. But every organization should be reconsidering and rethinking how it operates. Even before the current economic crisis, businesses were feeling pressured by their customers to deliver more for less. This means that companies have to learn to deliver more with less— less capital, less people, less resources of all types. The ability of an organization to execute—efficiently and effectively—will be its key, not just to survival but to growth. It's what competing in global markets demands and what technology now enables.

In good times and bad, superb execution can be a company's distinctive competitive quality. Your business may not be able to compete by having uniquely innovative products or services (not every company can be Apple). But it can compete by having a unique operating model. As you can see from the enterprises in this book, customers come back to businesses that know how to deliver on their promise.

That's why the next book in this series will focus on how companies achieve true operational excellence. Like *Outsmart!* and *Inspire!*, it will have a simple, direct title: *Deliver!* That's because delivering is what every successful business does every day, in good times as well as bad.

A

Ackerman, Elan, 48

adidas, 139

ASL (American Sign Language). *See* Two Little Hands
Productions case study

authenticity

importance of, 4-5, 19-21

maintaining, 150

of message, 103

auto industry, 153

avoiding incrementalism, 52

B

Beastie Boys, 143

Bertone, Antonio, 142

Big Green Egg® case study, 17, 122-132

Biomega, 145

Bolt, Usain, 145

Boston Search Group, 38

breaking standard business rules, 33

broad appeal of causes, 35

Brown, Alex, 112

Brown, Derek, 16, 112

Brown, Emilie, 16, 112

Buffett, Jimmy, 73

C

Candice Michelle, 83

causes

choosing, 35

staying true to, 35

CCRx plan (MemberHealth), 57-69

Centers for Medicare and Medicaid Services (CMS), 60

Chalayan, Hussein, 144

change, balancing with consistency, 149

channel partners, choosing, 135

Chase, Robin, 42

choices, importance of, 52

Chrysler, 153

Civic (Honda), 153

CMS (Centers for Medicare and Medicaid Services), 60

Coleman, Aaron, 16, 108-119

Coleman, Leah, 109-114

Coleman, Lucy, 113, 116

Coleman, Rachel, 16, 108-119

commercializing ideas, 121

complexity, simplifying

    case study: GoDaddy.com, 75-85

    identifying customers' unmet needs, 85

    providing extraordinary customer service, 86-88

    tracking metrics, 88

consistency, balancing with change, 149

Consumerist.com, 7

consumers, independence of, 8-10

convenience

    avoiding incrementalism, 52

    case study: Zipcar, 12, 39-49

    combining convenience with layered benefits, 51

    expanding to new customer markets, 53

identifying business partners, 53

identifying potential customers, 53

knowing what convenience means to your customers, 51

offering choices, 52

creativity, 35

credibility, 132

credit crisis, 152-154

customers, engaging

with authenticity, 19-21

being your own customer

case study: Big Green Egg®, 122-132

case study: Two Little Hands Productions, 108-119

choosing channel partners, 135

commercializing ideas, 121

credibility, 132

empathy, 119-120

exclusivity and mystique, 134

faith and perseverence, 135

keeping distance, 120

realism, 133-134

trusting intuition, 120

with causes, 33-36

    breaking standard business rules, 33

    case study: Stonyfield Farm, 23-32

    choosing causes with broad appeal, 35

    creativity, 34

    emotional links, 32

    reinforcing message repeatedly, 33

    samples and hands-on product experience, 34

    staying true to cause, 35

by combining fashion and sport

    balancing consistency and change, 149

    building on your past, 147

    case study: Puma, 139-147

    maintaining authenticity, 150

    playing underdog role, 150

    taking on competitors laterally, 148

    using outsiders to challenge insiders, 149

with convenience

    avoiding incrementalism, 52

    case study: Zipcar, 39-49

    combining convenience with layered benefits, 51

    expanding to new customer markets, 53

identifying business partners, 53

identifying potential customers, 53

knowing what convenience means to your customers, 51

offering choices, 52

with enthusiasm

case study: Big Green Egg®, 122-132

choosing channel partners, 135

credibility, 132

exclusivity and mystique, 134

faith and perseverence, 135

realism, 133-134

with honesty

balancing with pragmatism, 106

case study: Honest Tea, 90, 94-103

ensuring authenticity of message, 103

keeping promises, 105

tailoring message to market, 103-105

taking cue from customers, 105

by simplifying complexity

case study: GoDaddy.com, 75-85

identifying customers' unmet needs, 85

providing extraordinary customer service, 86-88

tracking metrics, 88

through trusted channels

assuring benefits to all players, 71

case study: MemberHealth, 56-69

focusing on end customer, 71

giving away something for free, 72

helping channel customers deliver more to partners, 70

knowing your customers and channel partners, 69-70

layering benefits to keep customers engaged, 72

handshake with the customer, 27

customer service, importance of, 86-88

D

Dal-Tile Corporation, 127

Darwin, Charles, 3, 152

Dassler, Adolf, 139

Dassler, Rudolf, 139

Denton, Nick, 7

DHM Group, Inc., 130

Disney EPCOT Center Land Pavilion, 23

E

economic slowdown, 152-154

Eggheads (Big Green Egg community), 131

Eggtoberfest, 132

emotional links, encouraging, 32

empathy, 119-120

engaging customers

with authenticity, *19-21*

being your own customer

case study: Big Green Egg®, 122-132

case study: Two Little Hands Productions, 108-119

choosing channel partners, 135

commercializing ideas, 121

credibility, 132

empathy, 119-120

exclusivity and mystique, 134

faith and perseverance, 135

keeping distance, 120

realism, 133-134

trusting intuition, 120

with causes, 33-36

breaking standard business rules, 33

case study: Stonyfield Farm, 23-32

choosing causes with broad appeal, 35

creativity, 34

emotional links, 32

reinforcing message repeatedly, 33

samples and hands-on product experience, 34

staying true to cause, 35

by combining fashion and sport

balancing consistency and change, 149

building on your past, 147

case study: Puma, 139-147

maintaining authenticity, 150

playing underdog role, 150

taking on competitors laterally, 148

using outsiders to challenge insiders, 149

with convenience

avoiding incrementalism, 52

case study: Zipcar, 39-49

combining convenience with layered benefits, 51

expanding to new customer markets, 53

identifying business partners, 53

identifying potential customers, 53

knowing what convenience means to your customers, 51

offering choices, 52

with enthusiasm

case study: Big Green Egg®, 122-132

choosing channel partners, 135

credibility, 132

exclusivity and mystique, 134

faith and perseverence, 135

realism, 133-134

with honesty

balancing with pragmatism, 106

case study: Honest Tea, 90-103

ensuring authenticity of message, 103

keeping promises, 105

tailoring message to market, 103-105

taking cue from customers, 105

by simplifying complexity

case study: GoDaddy.com, 75-85

identifying customers' unmet needs, 85

providing extraordinary customer service, 86-88

tracking metrics, 88

through trusted channels

assuring benefits to all players, 71

case study: MemberHealth, 56-69

focusing on end customer, 71

giving away something for free, 72

helping channel customers deliver more to partners, 70

knowing your customers and channel partners, 69-70

layering benefits to keep customers engaged, 72

handshake with the customer, 27-29

EPCOT Center Land Pavilion, 23

Evisu, 144

exclusivity, 134

F

Fair Trade drink (Honest Tea), 97

fashion, combining with sport

balancing consistency and change, 149

building on your past, 147

case study: Puma, 139-147

maintaining authenticity, 150

playing underdog role, 150

taking on competitors laterally, 148

using outsiders to challenge insiders, 149

Fisher, Ed, 17, 122-132

Flexcar, 41. *See also* Zipcar

Frazier, Walter, 143

Fresh Fields, 95

G

give-aways, 72

global economic slowdown, 152-154

GoDaddy.com case study, 75-85

Golden Buckeye Card, 59

Goldman, Seth, 90-103

Griffith, Scott, 43-48

H

Haarlem Honeybush tea (Honest Tea), 97

Hallberg, Charles, 13, 56-69

handshake with customer, 27-29

hands-on product experience, 34

Hirshberg, Gary, 12, 22-26, 31

Home Depot, 153

Honda, 153

Honest Kids juice pouches (Honest Tea), 101

Honest Tea case study, 15, 90-103

honesty

    balancing with pragmatism, 106

    case study: Honest Tea, 90-103

    ensuring authenticity of message, 103

    keeping promises, 105

    tailoring message to market, 103-105

    taking cue from customers, 105

honeybush tea, 97

I

ICANN (Internet Corporation for Assigned Names and Numbers), 79

idealism, 106

identifying

    customers' unmet needs, 85

    potential customers, 53

IKEA, sponsorship of Zipcar, 49

incrementalism, avoiding, 52

independence of consumers, 8-10

insiders, challenging outsiders with, 149

Internet Corporation for Assigned Names and Numbers (ICANN), 79

intuition, 120

J

Johnson & Johnson, Tylenol recall, 20

Jomax, 78

Jomax Technologies, 75

Jones Soda, 103

K

kamado. *See* Big Green Egg® case study

Kaymen, Louise, 27

Kaymen, Samuel, 26-32

keeping promises, 105

Kraft Foods, 23

L

Lampedusa, Giuseppe di, 148

Land Pavilion (EPCOT Center), 23

layered benefits, combining with convenience, 51

The Leopard (Lampedusa), 148

M

Madonna, 143

Malloy, Matthew, 43

Maradona, Diego, 143

marketing campaigns, limitations of, 10

McQueen, Alexander, 144

Medicare Modernization Act of 2003, 57

Medicare Part D prescription drug program, partnership with MemberHealth, 57-69

MemberHealth case study, 13-14, 56-69

message

authenticity of, 103

tailoring to market, 103-105

metrics, tracking, 88

Michaud, Christina, 47

Mohawk Industries, 127

Mongolian Shoe BBQ, 145

mystique, 134

N

Nalebuff, Barry, 90-103

Namath, Joe, 143

Nascimento, Edison Arantes do (Pelé), 143

NCPA (National Community Pharmacists Association), 61

New Alchemy Institute, 23

O

outsiders, challenging insiders with, 149

Outsmart! (Champy), 3, 21

Owens, Jesse, 140

P

Parsons, Bob, 74-75

Parsons Technology, 78

Part D prescription drug program, partnership with
  MemberHealth, 57-69

partnering with other organizations

    assuring benefits to all players, 71

    case study: Zipcar, 49-53

    focusing on end customer, 71

    giving away something for free, 72

    helping channel partners deliver more to customers, 70

    knowing your customers and channel partners, 69-70

    layering benefits to keep customers engaged, 72

    MemberHealth case study, 56-69

past, building on, 147

Patrick, Danica, 83

PBMs (prescription benefit management companies), 59

Pelé, 143

perseverence, 135

Pinault, Francois-Henri, 146

Popken, Ben, 6-7

pragmatism, 106

prescription benefit management companies (PBMs), 59

promises, keeping, 105

Puma case study, 139-147

R

realism, 133-134

recession, 152-154

reinforcing message, 33

Revco, 59

Roberts, Bruce, 61

Rogge, Jacque, 147

rules, breaking, 33

S

samples, 34

Sander, Jil, 143

S. C. Johnson Company, 20

Show Me a Sign, 115

Signing Time—My First Signs, 115

sign language. *See* Two Little Hands Productions case study

simplifying complexity

    case study: GoDaddy.com, 75-85

    identifying customers' unmet needs, 85

    providing extraordinary customer service, 86-88

    tracking metrics, 88

Smith & Wesson, 147

Stark, Philippe, 144

staying true to cause, 35

Stonyfield Farm case study, 12, 23-32

T

tailoring message to market, 103-105

taking on competitors laterally, 148

Tata Tea Company, 91

Tazo, 103

Thrift (Puma), 145

tracking metrics, 88

traditional marketing campaigns, limitations of, 10

trusted channels

assuring benefits to all players, 71

focusing on end customer, 71

giving away something for free, 72

helping channel customers deliver more to partners, 70

knowing your customers and channel partners, 69-70

layering benefits to keep customers engaged, 72

MemberHealth case study, 56-69

Turlington, Christy, 144

Two Little Hands Productions case study, 16, 108-119

Tylenol recall, 20

U

underdog role, 150

UnitedHealthcare, 64

United States Agency for International Development (USAID), 97

Universal American Financial Corporation, 68

unmet needs of customers, identifying, 85

USAID (United States Agency for International Development), 97

V-W

Vexed Generation, 145

Waterfall, Clark, 38

Website Tonight, 79

Whole Foods Markets, 95

Williams, Serena, 144

X-Y-Z

Yasuhiro, Mihara, 144

yogurt, organic, 26

Zeitz, Jochen, 139-147

Zero drink (Honest Tea), 96

Zipcar, 12, 39-49

Zipsters, 41